ESOP ECONOMICS
REPURCHASE OBLIGATION EXPERTS

°TELESCOPE°
THE #1 REPURCHASE OBLIGATION SOFTWARE

UPCOMING EDUCATIONAL WEBINARS

APRIL 21, 2016 3PM ET

Benefit Levels and ESOP Sustainability
Do high benefit levels make your ESOP unsustainable? Not necessarily!

Managing & Funding Repurchase Obligations
Understanding the implications of your ESOP distribution and funding decisions

JUNE 23, 2016 3PM ET

AUG 11, 2016 3PM ET

Redeeming vs. Recycling
An in-depth examination of the two basic repurchase methods

Can We Afford This ESOP?
Integrating repurchase obligation projections into a financial model to answer the three important questions about ESOP durability

OCT 20, 2016 3PM ET

Each webinar will include a brief demonstration of our Telescope software.
Learn More: www.esopeconomics.com/telescope

CONTACT US TO REGISTER:
info@esopeconomics.com
(215) 606-3600

CORPORATION
ESOPs

FOURTH EDITION

KATHRYN F. ASCHWALD · BARBARA M. CLOUGH
BRIAN HECTOR · MATTHEW G. KEENE · THOMAS ROBACK, JR.
COREY ROSEN · DONNA J. WALKER · CAROLYN F. ZIMMERMAN

THE NATIONAL CENTER FOR EMPLOYEE OWNERSHIP · OAKLAND, CALIFORNIA

S Corporation ESOPs, 4th ed.

Book design by Scott Rodrick

The National Center for Employee Ownership
Phone (510) 208-1300
Fax (510) 272-9510
www.nceo.org

First edition, July 2004; second edition, October 2005; third edition, March 2008, reprinted March 2010 ; fourth edition, November 2014

ISBN: 978-1-938220-22-7

Contents

Preface

An employee stock ownership plan (ESOP) is a powerful tool that can greatly benefit both employees and their employer. When an ESOP owns an S corporation, it is partially or wholly exempt from federal income taxation (and possibly state taxation, depending on the state), making it an even more powerful tool in many cases. With the tax-planning possibilities offered by the S corporation ESOP structure, many S corporations have adopted ESOPs, many C corporations with ESOPs have elected S status, and many non-ESOP companies are investigating ESOPs and S corporate status. But there are crucial issues to deal with along the way, ranging from valuation issues to matters that arise when making the S corporation election (if the company is not already an S corporation) to dealing with the unavailability of the tax-deferred ESOP "rollover" for S corporation owners. And it is absolutely imperative for any company considering or maintaining an S corporation ESOP to test its compliance with the strict anti-abuse rules for S corporation ESOPs.

This book deals with all these issues and more in a clear and understandable style. This fourth edition has been updated throughout, with every chapter either being updated or (in the case of chapter 7) replaced. Additionally, a new chapter at the end of the book addresses the increasingly important and much-discussed topic of creating a sustainable ESOP company. For more information on these and other employee ownership topics, visit us online at www.nceo.org.

Chapter 1

How ESOPs Work

Corey Rosen

An ESOP is a kind of employee benefit plan. Governed by ERISA (the Employee Retirement Income Security Act), ESOPs were given a specific statutory framework in 1974. ESOPs are similar in many ways to 401(k) plans and profit sharing plans. All of these plans operate through a trust, require that their benefits be provided on a nondiscriminatory basis to employees, and provide both the sponsoring employer and the employee with significant tax benefits. Unlike 401(k) plans, however, ESOPs are almost invariably funded entirely by the company, and, unlike all other retirement plans, they are intended to be invested primarily in employer securities. They also are unique in their ability to borrow money. ESOPs are not stock options (an entirely different way to share equity), nor can they be used to deliver stock just to selected employees, even on the basis of merit.

As of 2014, there were close to 7,000 ESOPs covering about 13 million participants and holding about 1 trillion dollars in assets. ESOPs have thus become a significant part of the U.S. economy. They can be found in companies ranging in size from a handful of employees to hundreds of thousands. Their most common application, however, is in small to mid-sized privately held companies with at least 15 employees.

ESOPs have been granted a number of tax benefits that go beyond those normally available to retirement plans. Congress has seen the growth of broad ownership as good economic and social policy, a view that has been borne out by research showing that ESOPs generally enhance corporate performance and employee financial security, often substantially. ESOPs, of course, are not some magical elixir that need only be imbibed under an attorney's directions to produce magical effects. Successful ESOP companies work hard to integrate employees as owners, sharing information and work-level decision making with them in an effort to create a true ownership culture.

ESOP Applications

ESOPs are used for a wide variety of purposes:

- The most common application for an ESOP is to buy the shares of a departing owner of a closely held company. In C corporations, owners can defer taxes on the gain they make from the sale to an ESOP if the ESOP holds 30% or more of the company's stock and certain other requirements are met. Moreover, the purchase can be made in pretax corporate dollars. S corporations are often converted to C corporations before the sale, although with historically low capital gains rates, many S corporation owners choose to retain S status and go ahead and pay taxes now.

- ESOPs are also used to divest or acquire subsidiaries, buy back shares from the market (such as in the case of public companies seeking takeover defenses), or restructure existing benefit plans by replacing current benefit contributions with a leveraged ESOP (i.e., one that borrows money, as described later in this chapter).

- ESOPs can purchase newly issued shares in the company, with the borrowed funds being used to buy new productive capital or finance an acquisition. The company can, in effect, finance growth or acquisitions in pretax dollars while these same dollars create an employee benefit plan.

- The above uses generally involve borrowing money through the ESOP, but a company can simply contribute new shares of stock to an ESOP, or cash to buy existing shares, as a means to create an employee benefit plan. As more and more companies want to find ways to link employee and corporate interests, this is becoming a more popular application. In public companies especially, an ESOP contribution is often used as part or all of a match to employee deferrals to a 401(k) plan.

Different Tax Benefits for S and C Corporation ESOPs

In return for agreeing to fund the ESOP, the company gets a number of tax benefits, provided it follows the rules to assure employees are treated fairly. While some of these are the same for S and C corporation ESOPs, some differ. Table 1-1 provides details. The rest of the chapter explains each of these features and their requirements.

Table 1-1. Tax issues for S and C corporation ESOPs		
Tax issue	S corporation ESOP	C corporation ESOP
Deferral of capital gains tax for sale to ESOP under Section 1042 is available	No	Yes (if Section 1042 rules are met)
Company does not pay federal or, usually, state income tax on share of profits attributable to the ESOP	Yes	Company pays taxes on all its profits regardless of how much the ESOP owns
Dividends paid on ESOP shares are deductible	No (S corporations do not pay dividends, and distributions are not deductible)	Yes, if used to repay an ESOP loan, passed through to employees, or voluntarily reinvested by employees in company stock
Contributions to the ESOP, either directly or to repay the ESOP debt, are deductible up to 25% of covered payroll	Both interest and principal payments count toward the 25% limit	Only payments toward principal must be counted toward 25% of covered payroll
Forfeitures of unvested account balances from departed employees count toward limit on maximum annual additions to employee accounts (100% of pay or $52,000 [as of 2014]; includes all employer and employee contributions to retirement plans)	Yes	No
Distributions of account balances for departed participants can be delayed until after ESOP loan is repaid	No	Yes
In calculating the maximum amount that can go into a leveraged ESOP, employer contributions to other qualified retirement plans do not count	No	Yes

Financing an ESOP

A significant minority of ESOPs are funded by contributions of cash to the plan or, less often, by companies contributing newly issued shares. In new ESOPs, cash contributions are usually used to buy existing shares from an owner or owners. The company can also put cash in for some period of time, probably a few years, to build up a cash reserve to make a significant purchase of stock. As ESOPs mature, many companies make cash contributions to the ESOP, which the plan uses to create a reserve to buy shares back from employees. Each participant ends up with a stock account and a cash account within the plan. If the company simply contributes shares, it can take a tax deduction for them even though there is no immediate cash expense. Owners cannot contribute shares directly to the plan, however. In any direct contribution approach, each participant is credited with an allocation of his or her share of the contribution when it is made.

Even more rare is the use of existing employee money to help fund the ESOP. Most often, this comes from a voluntary transfer of 401(k) funds. Such transfers are subject to securities laws requirements and must meet strict ERISA rules for financial disclosure and prudence. Because compliance is very expensive, this approach is only used in large transactions needing an equity infusion.

The most common and powerful way to finance an ESOP, however, is to borrow money (a "leveraged ESOP"). The ESOP can borrow money from anyone, including commercial lenders, sellers of stock, or even the company itself. In this approach, the company sets up a trust, which then borrows money from a lender. The company repays the loan by making tax-deductible contributions to the trust that the trust gives to the lender. The trust must use the loan to acquire stock in the company. The company can use proceeds from the loan for any legitimate business purpose. Any loan to an ESOP must meet several requirements, however. It must have reasonable rates and terms, and it must be repaid only from employer contributions, dividends on shares in the plan, and earnings from other investments in the trust contributed by the employer. There is no limit on the term of an ESOP loan other than what lenders will accept (normally five to ten years).

A best practice for ESOP loans is to have the lender loan to the company, not the ESOP. Then company then reloans that money to the

ESOP, which uses the funds to buy shares from the seller. There are four major benefits to this approach:

- First, the ESOP can only offer company stock as collateral. If the company loses value, the collateral (i.e., its stock) loses value as well. In contrast, the company can offer assets as collateral. In many cases, the shareholder(s) selling to the ESOP will also back up the loan.

- Second, the terms of the two loans (lender to company vs. company to ESOP) do not have to be the same. Suppose that the loan term is short because the company wants to repay the loan fairly quickly. In that case, if the lender loans directly to the ESOP, the shares will be allocated quickly (because they are allocated as the loan is repaid). By having the company borrow the money and having a longer term for the "inside" loan it makes to the ESOP than for the "outside" loan between the lender and the company, the ESOP allocations can be spread over a correspondingly longer period, which will be fairer to new employees who become participants after some of the stock allocations have already been made.

- Third, the term of the loan from an outside lender might necessitate annual payments so high that the legal limits on annual contributions to defined contribution plans would be exceeded if the loan were directly to the ESOP. The company can avoid this by borrowing from the lender and then making a loan with a longer term to the ESOP.

- Finally, ERISA rules make it easier to restructure a loan to the company, such as in a potential default situation, than a loan to an ESOP.

In recent years, seller financing for all or part of the purchase price has become increasingly popular, although bank loans are still very common and banks generally have a positive view of ESOPs, which have a very low default rate. With seller financing, the seller takes a note over typically five to seven years. The rate of interest must be the equivalent of an arms-length rate for loans of similar risk (in recent years, this has typically been 5% to 9%). In some cases, sellers take a lower interest rate but also get warrants they can redeem in the future if the share value goes up. Because the rate of return on these notes is attractive relative to other uses for the proceeds from the sale, seller financing can be very appealing. However, if the company starts out as a C corporation and the seller wants to elect Section 1042 tax-deferred treatment (discussed below) for the gain, a seller note requires a more complicated reinvestment strategy to comply with the rules.

Shares in the plan are held in a suspense account. As the loan is repaid, these shares are released to the accounts of plan participants. The release must follow one of two formulas. The simpler of the two is the "principal-only" method, in which the percentage of shares released equals the percentage of principal paid, either that year or during whatever shorter repayment period is used. In such cases, however, the release may not be slower than what normal amortization schedules would provide for a 10-year loan with level payments of principal and interest. The principal-only method usually has the effect of releasing fewer shares to participants in the early years. Alternatively, the company can base its release on the total amount of principal and interest it pays each year. This method can be used for any loan, but it must be used for loans of more than 10 years. After employees leave the company or retire, the company distributes to them the stock purchased on their behalf, or its cash value. In practice, banks often insist on making the loan to the company instead of the trust, with the company re-loaning the proceeds to the ESOP.

In either case, it is important to remember that the value of the shares released each year is rarely the same as the amount contributed to repay the principal on the loan. If the price of the shares goes up, the amount released will be higher in dollar terms than the amount contributed; if it goes down, the dollar value of the amount released will be lower. The amount *contributed* to repay the principal on the loan is what counts for determining whether the company is within the limits for contributions allowed each year and for the purpose of calculating the tax deduction. The value of the shares released, however, is the amount used for accounting purposes on the income statement, where it counts as a compensation cost.

Dividends (in C corporations) or distributions (in S corporations) can also be used to repay the debt. These are tax deductible in C corporations, but not in S (albeit this is not an issue for 100% S ESOPs that pay no taxes). The dividends or distributions release shares that have not yet been paid for into employee accounts, either on the basis of the pro-rata share of each employee's share account balance to the total shares in the plan or the company's normal compensation formula. For shares already in employee accounts, dividends or distributions would be used to pay for additional shares from the suspense account based on the employee's pro-rata share balance.

S corporations sometimes also use distributions paid to an ESOP to buy additional shares, even if these are not used to repay a loan. In an S corporation, distributions are normally made to owners so they can pay their share of income taxes on corporate profits. By law, any distributions must go pro-rata to all owners. So if the ESOP owns 30% of the stock, it must get 30% of the distributions. The ESOP can simply allocate this added cash to employee accounts (based on each employee's pro-rata share of the account balances) or use them to buy more shares. One disadvantage of this approach is that it means those employees with existing account balances get more and more shares, while newer employees get relatively less, or even nothing if no direct contributions to the ESOP are made. While some owners are happy with this approach, more often it causes problems in that there now are two classes of employees. In some cases, the approach can even cause companies to violate the "anti-abuse" rules described in detail later in this book. These problems can be avoided with good advice from counsel.

Limits on Contributions

In 2001, Congress made significant changes to contribution limits in all employee retirement plans, governed by Section 404 of the Internal Revenue Code. The new rules significantly raised these limits so that they are rarely an issue in ESOPs. Understanding two basic concepts will make these limits more intelligible. The first is "eligible pay." This refers to the compensation, either on an individual or aggregate basis, that can be counted in making contributions. Pay over certain amounts, the pay of "disqualified" individuals, and the pay of employees not yet participating in the plan are all examples of ineligible pay. The second is "annual additions." This refers to the amounts that are added to employee accounts in a year through corporate contributions and individual deferrals into retirement plans. Limits on annual additions to plans are covered by Section 415 of the Internal Revenue Code, so these limits are often called "Section 415 limits." Finally, a separate set of limits applies to how much a company can deduct when contributing to an ESOP or another retirement plan.

It is important to understand that for purposes of calculating the Section 415 limits in a leveraged ESOP, the amount that is defined as an "annual addition" to an employee's account is based on the amount the company contributed that year to repay that portion of the loan (either principal only or principal and interest, depending on the share release method used) attributable to the shares added to the employee's account. The actual value of the shares added to the employee's account, however, is usually different (e.g., if the per-share price is higher than at the time of purchase, the value of the shares added to the account will be higher than the amount defined as the "annual addition").

Generally, companies can deduct up to 25% of the total eligible payroll of plan participants to cover the principal portion of the loan and can deduct all of the interest they pay. Eligible pay includes all W-2 compensation plus employee deferrals into benefit plans, but only for employees actually in the plan. Pay over $260,000 per participant (as of 2014[1]) is not eligible. Company contributions to other defined contribution plans, such as stock bonus, 401(k), or profit sharing plans, must be counted in this 25% of pay calculation. On the other hand, "reasonable" dividends paid on shares acquired by a C corporation ESOP can be used to repay the loan and are not included in the 25% of pay calculations. Dividends in C corporations that are passed through to employees or passed through and voluntarily reinvested in company stock are also deductible beyond the 25% limit. In a C corporation, if employees leave the company before they have a fully vested right to their ESOP shares, their forfeitures, which are allocated to everyone else, are not counted in the percentage limitations in leveraged ESOPs. If the ESOP does not borrow money, the annual contribution limit is also 25% of covered pay. Employer (but not employee) contributions to other plans reduce this amount.

In C corporations, there are separate 25% limits for (1) contributions to pay principal on an ESOP loan and (2) contributions to other

---

1. This and other dollar limits designated here as being "as of 2014" are increased annually for inflation.

defined contribution plans; thus, a company with a leveraged ESOP and a profit sharing plan, for example, has a 50% total limit (up to 25% for a leveraged ESOP plus up to 25% for other defined contribution plans such as the profit sharing plan). However, in S corporations, company contributions to both leveraged ESOPs and other defined contribution plans all fall under a single 25% of eligible pay calculation.

The above limits are for deductibility of aggregate corporate contributions; a separate set of limits applies to annual additions to individual employee accounts. First, no one ESOP participant can get more than 100% of pay in any year from company contributions to the ESOP, or more than $52,000 (as of 2014), whichever is less. In figuring payroll, pay over $260,000 per year (as of 2014) does not count toward total contribution limits.

Second, other qualified benefit plans must be taken into account when assessing this annual addition limit. This means that employee deferrals into 401(k) plans, as well as employer contributions to 401(k), stock bonus, or profit sharing plans, are added to the ESOP contribution and cannot exceed 100% of pay in any year.

Third, the interest on an ESOP loan is excludable from the 25% of pay individual limit in C corporations only if not more than one-third of the benefits are allocated to "highly compensated employees," as defined by the Internal Revenue Code (Section 414(q)). If the one-third rule is not met, forfeitures in C corporations are also counted in determining how much an employee is getting each year. If the company sponsoring the ESOP is an S corporation, interest is also not deductible, and forfeitures do count toward the 25% of pay limit.

How Shares Get to Employees

The rules for ESOPs are similar to the rules for other tax-qualified plans in terms of participation, allocation, vesting, and distribution, but several special considerations apply. All employees over age 21 who work for more than 1,000 hours in a plan year must be included, unless they are covered by a collective bargaining unit, are in a separate line of business with at least 50 employees not covered by the ESOP, or fall under one of several anti-discrimination exemptions not commonly used by ESOPs. If there is a union, the company must bargain in good faith with it over inclusion in the plan.

Shares are allocated to individual employee accounts based on relative compensation (generally, all W-2 compensation is counted), on a more level formula (such as per capita or seniority), or some combination thereof. The allocated shares are subject to vesting. Employees must be 100% vested after three years of service, or the company can use a graduated vesting schedule not slower than 20% after two years and 20% per year more until 100% is reached after six years. A faster vesting schedule applies where the ESOP contribution is used as a match to employee 401(k) deferrals. There, "cliff" vesting must be complete in three years, and graduated vesting must start after two years and be completed no later than after six years.

When employees reach age 55 and have 10 years of participation in the plan, the ESOP must either give them the option during the following five years of diversifying 25% of their account balances among at least three other investment alternatives or simply pay the amount out to the employees. During the sixth year, employees can have a cumulative total of 50% diversified or distributed to them.

When employees retire, die, or are disabled, the company must distribute their vested shares to them or their heirs not later than the last day of the plan year following the year of the departure. For employees leaving before reaching retirement age, distribution must begin not later than the last day of the sixth plan year following the year of separation from service. C corporations can delay this distribution to terminated employees (other than for death, retirement, or disability) until after the ESOP loan is repaid. Payments can be in substantially equal installments out of the trust over five years, or in a lump sum. In the installment method, a company normally pays out a portion of the stock from the trust each year. The value of that stock may go up or down over that time, of course. In a lump-sum distribution, the company buys the shares at their current value, but it can make the purchase in installments over five years, as long as it provides adequate security and reasonable interest. ESOP shares must be valued at least annually by an independent outside appraiser unless the shares are publicly traded.

Closely held companies and some thinly traded public companies must repurchase the shares from departing employees at their fair market value, as determined by an independent appraiser. This "put option" can be exercised by the employee in one of two 60-day periods, one starting when the employee receives the distribution and the second period one year after that. The employee can choose which one to use. This obligation should be considered at the outset of the ESOP and factored into the company's ability to repay the loan.

Voting Rules

Voting is one of the most controversial and least understood of ESOP issues. The trustee of the ESOP actually votes the ESOP shares. The question is, "Who directs the trustee?" The trustee can make the decision independently, although that is very rare. Alternatively, management or the ESOP administrative committee can direct the trustee, or the trustee can follow employee directions.

In private companies, employees must be able to direct the trustee as to the voting of shares *allocated* to their accounts on several key issues, including closing, sale, liquidation, recapitalization, and other issues having to do with the basic structure of the company. They do not, however, have to be able to vote for the board of directors or on other typical corporate governance issues, although companies can voluntarily provide these rights. Instead, the plan trustee votes the shares, usually at the direction of management. In public companies, employees must be able to vote on all issues.

Voting rights are more complicated than they seem. First, voting is not the same as tendering shares. So while employees may be required to be able to vote on all issues, they may have no say about whether shares are tendered. In public companies, this is a major issue.

Second, employers are not required to allow employees to vote on unallocated shares. In a leveraged ESOP, this means that for the first several years of the loan, the trustee can vote the majority of the shares, if that is what the company wants to do. The company could provide that unallocated shares, as well as any allocated shares for which the trustee has not received instructions, should be voted or tendered in proportion to the allocated shares for which directions were received.

What this all means is that for almost all ESOP companies, governance is not really an issue unless they want it to be. If companies want employees to have only the most limited role in corporate governance, they can; if they want to go beyond this, they can as well. In practice, companies that do provide employees with a substantial governance role find that it does not result in dramatic changes in the way the company is run.

Valuation

In closely held companies and some thinly traded public companies, every ESOP transaction must be based on a current appraisal by an independent, outside valuation expert. The valuation process assesses how much a willing buyer would pay a willing seller for the business. This calculation is performed by looking at, among other things, various ratios, such as the price-to-earnings ratio; at discounted future cash flow and earnings; at asset value; and at the market value of comparable companies. It is then adjusted to reflect whether the sale is for control (owning a controlling interest in a business is worth more than owning a minority interest, even on a per-share basis) and marketability (shares of public companies are worth more than shares of closely held companies because public company shares are easier to buy and sell). ESOP company shares have better marketability than those of non-ESOP companies, however, because the ESOP provides a market, albeit not as active a market as a stock exchange. The appraisal must be performed by an independent, outside appraiser (one without another business relationship with the company) working for the ESOP trust, not the company. The appraiser determines the maximum the ESOP can pay; in some cases, the ESOP trustee may argue that the price should or could be lower and negotiate for that better price.

Fiduciary Issues

Like other tax-qualified retirement plans, an ESOP must have a trustee who makes decisions concerning plan assets. The most important decisions concern voting ESOP shares, deciding whether the ESOP is paying not more than fair market value, deciding whether to tender shares in an acquisition offer or merger, and making sure the plan's administration follows plan and statutory rules. The trustee may take directions from another party, such as the board, employees (when companies pass through voting or tendering decisions), or management, however.

The individual or entity making decisions is always considered the plan fiduciary and is legally responsible for how those decisions are made. If the trustee is directed by a third party acting as fiduciary, then the trustee has less of a fiduciary responsibility but still must make sure that decisions are in compliance with the law and plan documents. Fiduciaries should be indemnified by the company and insured, as they are personally responsible in the case of adverse judgments. In evaluating whether a fiduciary performed his or her duties, courts look to the process more than the results. At the time a decision is made, fiduciaries should, at the least:

- Rely on qualified, independent advice from experienced ESOP advisors;

- Conduct an independent evaluation of the issue and make a prudent decision based on the best interests of plan participants as participants in a benefit plan, rather than solely as employees of the company;

- Not be in a conflict-of-interest situation, such as a seller would be in judging whether the ESOP is paying a fair price for his or her stock; and

- Be knowledgeable about the law and current best practices.

Most larger companies hire independent trustees to act as fiduciaries. These trustees provide a kind of insurance, because courts tend to ascribe more credibility to the independence and judgment of a fiduciary who is an experienced outside expert. Outside trustees are costly, however, so most smaller companies use corporate officers (other than the sellers) or committees of employees, sometimes including nonmanagement employees.

Tax Benefits to the Selling Shareholder

One of the major benefits of an ESOP for a closely held company is Section 1042 of the Internal Revenue Code. Under it, a seller to an ESOP may be able to qualify for a deferral of taxation on the gain made from the sale. Several requirements apply, the most significant of which are:

1. The seller must have held the stock for three years before the sale.

2. The stock must not have been acquired through options or other employee benefit plans.

3. The ESOP must own 30% or more of the value of the shares in the company and must continue to hold this amount for three years unless the company is sold. Shares repurchased by the company from departing employees do not count. Stock sold in a transaction that brings the ESOP to 30% of the total shares qualifies for the deferral treatment.

4. Shares qualifying for the deferral cannot be allocated to accounts of children, brothers or sisters, spouses, or parents of the selling shareholder(s), or to other 25% shareholders.

5. The company must be a C corporation.

If these rules are met, the sellers can take the proceeds from the sale and reinvest them in "qualified replacement property" between 3 months before and 12 months after the sale and defer any capital gains taxes until these new investments are sold. Qualified replacement property is defined essentially as stocks, bonds, warrants, or debentures of domestic corporations receiving not more than 25% of their income from passive investment. Mutual funds and real estate trusts do not qualify. If the replacement property is held until death, they are subject to a step-up in basis, so capital gains taxes are never due.

Increasingly, lenders are asking for the replacement property as part or all of the collateral for an ESOP loan. This strategy may be beneficial to sellers selling only part of their holdings because it frees the corporation to use its assets for other borrowing and could enhance the future value of the company.

It is also important to note that people taking advantage of the 1042 treatment cannot have stock reallocated to their accounts from these sales if they remain employees. More-than-25% shareholders and close relatives of the seller also cannot receive allocations from these sales.

As noted earlier, sellers in S corporations cannot receive this tax benefit. Many S corporations convert to C status before selling to the ESOP, then may reconvert to S status after the loan is repaid (reconversion cannot occur sooner than five years after leaving S status, however). During the period when the acquisition loan is being repaid, deductions often eliminate much or even all of the income tax obligation, so S status is less important. Other owners, however, choose to retain S status. They may have relatives they want to be in the plans, or they may want to stay in the plan themselves if they are still working. There may also be more-than-25% shareholders who cannot elect Section 1042 tax-deferred treatment. Some owners would prefer to pay taxes now and not be limited in what they can reinvest in. With the top federal capital gains tax rate at 20%, plus both a 3.8% additional Medicare tax on investment income above a certain threshold and, often, state taxes, the ability to defer taxation is more important than it was before tax law changes in 2013, however. Other reasons that may make S-to-C conversion unwise include:

- *There are large amounts of undistributed earnings.* When the conversion to a C corporation takes place, any earnings that have not yet been contributed to the owners must be distributed in one year or they are taxable to the owners (meaning they will be taxed twice, since the owners have already paid tax on them before). If the company does not have the cash to do this, it could borrow money, but the ESOP may itself require too much cash to make this payout practical.

- *Remaining owners plan to sell the company in an asset sale some time after the ESOP is implemented.* In an S corporation, the sale of the company's assets triggers only a single tax at the individual level; in a C corporation, the sale would be taxed at both the corporate and individual level, as income to the company and as capital gains to the individuals. The amount of the corporate tax would depend in part on the depreciation taken on the assets.

- *The S corporation is creating losses the owners want flowed through to them.* In some situations, a company may be making heavy investments, often in real property or other hard assets, that create paper losses. These losses can be flowed through to the owners, who can deduct them at a marginally higher rate than can the company. In some scenarios, this may be desirable.

- *The seller's basis is already very high* because of taxes paid on previously undistributed earnings. In this case, the Section 1042 "rollover" provision may not make much difference.

Financial Issues for Employees

When an employee receives a distribution from the plan, it is taxable unless rolled over into an IRA or other qualified plan. Otherwise, the amounts contributed by the employer are taxable as ordinary income, while any appreciation on the shares is taxable as capital gains. In addition, if the employee receives the distribution before normal retirement age and does not roll over the funds, a 10% excise tax is added.

While the stock is in the plan, however, it is not taxable to employees. It is rare, moreover, for employees to give up wages to participate in an ESOP or to purchase stock directly through a plan (this raises difficult securities law issues for closely held companies). Most ESOPs either are in addition to existing benefit plans or replace other defined contribution plans, usually at a higher level of pay.

Determining ESOP Feasibility

Several factors are involved in determining whether a company is a good ESOP candidate:

- *Is the cost reasonable?* ESOPs typically cost $60,000 and up to implement, depending on complexity and the size of the transaction. This is usually much cheaper than other ways to sell a business, but more expensive than other benefit plans.

- *Is the payroll large enough?* Limitations on how much can be contributed to a plan may make it impractical to use to buy out a major owner or finance a large transaction. For instance, a $5 million purchase would not be feasible if the company has $500,000 of eligible payroll, because annual contributions could be no larger than $125,000 per year, not enough to repay a loan for that amount. Flexibility in the term of the ESOP loan, the ability to use dividends that do not count toward the limits (in C corporations), and the generous contribution limits available nowadays, however, make this problem relatively rare.

- *Can the company afford the contributions?* Many ESOPs are used to buy existing shares, a nonproductive expense. Companies need to assess whether they have the available earnings for this.

- *Is management comfortable with the idea of employees as owners?* While employees do not have to run the company, they will want more information and more say. Unless they are treated this way, research shows, they are likely to be demotivated by ownership.

The Repurchase Obligation

One of the major issues ESOPs must face is the obligation that closely held companies sponsoring them provide for the repurchase of shares of departing employees. The legal obligation rests with the company, although it can fund this by making tax-deductible contributions to the ESOP, which the ESOP uses to repurchase the shares. Most companies either do this or buy the shares back themselves and then recontribute them to the ESOP (and take a tax deduction for that). Either way, shares continue to circulate in the plan, providing stock for new employees. Some companies, however, buy back the shares and retire them or have other people buy them (a manager, for instance).

The repurchase obligation may seem like a reason not to do an ESOP ("You mean we have to buy back the shares continually?" people often ask). In fact, all closely held companies have a 100% repurchase obligation at all times. An ESOP simply puts it on a schedule and allows the company to do it in pretax dollars. Nonetheless, repurchase can be a major problem if companies do not anticipate and plan for it. A careful repurchase study should be done periodically to help manage this process.

Steps to Setting Up an ESOP

If you have decided an ESOP is worth investigating, there are several steps to take to implement a plan. At each point, you may decide that you have gone far enough and an ESOP is not right for you.

1. Determine Whether Other Owners Are Amenable

This may seem like an obvious issue, but sometimes people take several of the steps listed below before finding out whether all the existing owners are willing to sell. Employees should not start organizing a buyout unless they have some reason to think the parent firm is willing to sell (it may not be, for instance, if its goal is to reduce total output of a product it makes at other locations). Or there may be other owners of a private company who will never agree to an ESOP, even if it seems appealing to the principal owners. They could cause a good deal of trouble down the road.

2. Conduct a Feasibility Study

This may be a full-blown analysis by an outside consultant, replete with market surveys, management interviews, and detailed financial projections, or it may simply be a careful business plan performed in-house. Generally, full-scale feasibility studies are needed only where there is some doubt about the ESOP's ability to repay the loan. Any analysis, however, must look at several items. First, it must assess just how much extra cash flow the company has available to devote to the ESOP, and whether this is adequate for the purposes for which the ESOP is intended. Second, it must determine whether the company has adequate payroll for ESOP participants to make the ESOP contributions deductible. Remember to include the effect of other benefit plans that will be maintained in these calculations. Third, estimates must be made of the repurchase obligation (if the company is closely held) and thought given to how the company will handle it.

3. Conduct a Valuation

The feasibility study will rely on rough estimates of the value of the stock for the purpose of calculating the adequacy of cash and payroll. In private companies, this can be speculative. The next step for is a valuation. A company may want to have a preliminary valuation done first to see if the range of values produced is acceptable. A full valuation would follow if it is. Doing a valuation before implementing a plan is critical. If the value is too low, sellers may not be willing to sell. Or the price of the shares may be too high for the company to afford. The valuation consultant will look at a variety of factors, including cash flow, profits, market conditions, assets, comparable company values, goodwill, and overall economic factors. A discount on value may be taken if the ESOP is buying less than 50% of the shares.

4. Hire an ESOP Attorney

If the first three steps prove positive, the plan can now be drafted and submitted to the IRS. You should carefully evaluate your options and tell your attorney just how you want the ESOP to be set up. This could save you a considerable amount of money in consultation time. The IRS may take many months to issue you a "letter of determination" on your plan, but you can go ahead and start making contributions before then. If the IRS rules unfavorably, which rarely happens, normally you just need to amend your plan.

5. Obtain Funding for the Plan

We have previously discussed the variety of methods available for funding. Keep in mind that many plans combine approaches. Of particular note is the increase in seller-financed ESOPs. Although banks have generally been positive about ESOP lending, more sellers are choosing to take a note from the ESOP instead. This avoids the costs and potential delays of obtaining a bank loan. The note must be on terms at least as favorable as an arms-length equivalent transaction. The loan may be made directly to the ESOP or to the company, which reloans it to the ESOP. This allows the company to repay the loan to the seller on different terms than those with which the ESOP repays its loan to the company. One possible downside to seller financing is that the seller will receive a stream of payments over the years; yet, if the seller wishes to take advantage of the Section 1042 tax deferral, the seller must buy all the qualified replacement property within a year after the ESOP transaction, i.e., before the seller has received most of the money (assuming a multi-year loan).[2] Seller-financed transactions in C corporations that are

---

2. The qualified replacement property bought for the Section 1042 tax deferral need not be bought with the actual proceeds of the transaction, but many

designed to take advantage of the Section 1042 tax deferral are none-theless possible: the seller can borrow the money to buy the qualified replacement property within the statutory period (perhaps with the qualified replacement property itself serving as collateral).

6. Establish a Process for Operating the Plan

A trustee must be chosen to oversee the plan. In most private companies, this will be someone from inside the firm, but some private and most public companies hire outside trustees. An ESOP committee will direct the trustee. In most companies, this is made up of management people, but many ESOP firms allow at least some nonmanagement represen-tation. Finally, and most important, a process must be established to communicate to employees how the plan works and to get them more involved as owners. These issues are also addressed in more detail later in this book.

---

sellers do not have an equivalent amount of cash on hand.

Chapter 2

Legal Considerations for S Corporation ESOPs

Brian Hector[1]

A corporation that sponsors an employee stock ownership plan (ESOP) can obtain extraordinary tax savings by making the election to be treated as an "S corporation" for federal income tax purposes.[2] An S corporation generally is not subject to federal income tax on its earnings.[3] Instead, the tax on an S corporation's earnings flows through to its shareholders, regardless of whether the earnings are distributed to shareholders as dividends or retained in the corporation.[4] An important tax advantage of this treatment is that only one tax is imposed on the earnings of an S corporation. Regular or "C" corporations are subject to a "double tax"—once at the corporate level[5] and again at the shareholder level when the after-tax corporate earnings are distributed to the shareholders.[6]

---

1. Mr. Hector would like to acknowledge the work and assistance of Jason Ray, a senior attorney of Morgan, Lewis & Bockius LLP, in preparing this chapter. The original version of this chapter was written by David Ackerman.

2. Internal Revenue Code ("Code") § 1361(c)(6).

3. Code § 1363(a).

4. Code § 1366(a).

5. Code § 11.

6. Code § 301. The impact of the double tax was reduced by the Jobs and Growth Tax Relief Reconciliation Act of 2003, which reduced the maximum rate of tax on dividends to 15%. However, the American Taxpayer Relief Act of 2012 raised the long-term capital gains and qualifying dividends tax rate to 20% (from 15%) for taxpayers in the 39.6% tax bracket. In addition, the Health Care and Education Reconciliation Act of 2010 added a 3.8% Medicare surtax on certain individuals with "net investment income," which includes dividends and capital gains.

This chapter summarizes the rules relating to S corporation ESOPs, as set forth in the Internal Revenue Code of 1986 (the "Code"). This chapter also provides a brief analysis of situations where either an ESOP may be appropriate for an S corporation or where an existing ESOP company might benefit from making the S election. Finally, to provide a context for this discussion, this chapter concludes with a brief summary of how S corporations are taxed and the benefits of the S election.

The Applicable Tax Laws

Authorization of S Corporation ESOPs

To be eligible to make the S election, a corporation may not have more than 100 shareholders, and the corporation may have only one class of stock outstanding.[7] In addition, all shareholders must be U.S. citizens or U.S. residents, and they must be natural persons, estates, or certain types of trusts (including employee benefit trusts).[8] An employee benefit plan trust is treated as a single shareholder of an S corporation.[9] This is of critical importance because of the 100-shareholder limit for S corporations. If each participant in an employee benefit plan were treated as a shareholder of the plan sponsor, then many ESOP companies would be rendered ineligible to make the S election by reason of the 100-shareholder limit.

Exemption from Unrelated Business Income Tax

Shares of an S corporation held by an employee benefit trust generally are treated as an interest in an "unrelated trade or business," with the result that the trust's share of the S corporation's income generally is taken into account in computing the trust's unrelated business income tax (UBIT).[10] In addition, any gain or loss realized by an employee benefit trust in connection with the disposition of employer securities

---

7. Code § 1361(b)(1)(A), (D).

8. Code § 1361(b) (1)(B). For a more detailed discussion of the S corporation eligibility requirements, see discussion below at footnotes 119–28.

9. S. Rep. No.105-35, 105th Cong., 1st Sess. (1997).

10. Code § 512(e).

generally must be taken into account for this purpose.[11] However, there is a special exemption from the application of the unrelated business income tax to ESOPs that hold stock of an S corporation.[12]

Special Distribution Rules

Generally, participants in an ESOP are entitled to demand that their benefits be distributed to them in the form of stock of the sponsoring employer.[13] However, there is an exception to this rule: an S corporation that sponsors an ESOP may require the participants in the plan to take their benefits in the form of cash.[14] This exception enables S corporations that sponsor ESOPs to avoid involuntary terminations of the S election, which otherwise could arise in either of two ways. First, a participant might request that the shares of employer stock allocated to his or her account be rolled over to an individual retirement arrangement (IRA). An IRA is not eligible to own shares of an S corporation.[15] Second, over time, if enough participants in the plan elect to take their benefits in the form of employer shares, the 100-shareholder limit might be exceeded. These problems can be avoided by requiring the participants in the ESOP to take their benefits in the form of cash.[16]

---

11. Code § 512(e)(1)(B).

12. Code § 512(e)(3).

13. Code § 409(h)(1)(A). This right can be denied to ESOP participants if the articles of incorporation or bylaws of the ESOP company restrict the ownership of substantially all outstanding employer securities to employees or to a qualified retirement plan. Code § 409(h)(2).

14. Code § 409(h)(2).

15. Code § 1361(b)(1)(B). However, in PLR 200122034 (Feb. 28, 2001), the Internal Revenue Service (the "IRS") ruled that momentary ownership of S corporation stock by an IRA would not result in an involuntary termination of the corporation's S election where the stock had been received in a direct transfer from an ESOP and was subject to the requirement that it be immediately sold back to the sponsor of the ESOP. In Revenue Procedure 2004-14, the IRS held that it was permissible for the ESOP trust, as well as for the plan sponsor, to buy the shares.

16. Code § 409(h)(2).

Inapplicability of Certain C Corporation Tax Incentives

Some of the tax incentives that have been provided for C corporations that adopt ESOPs do not apply to S corporations:

- Upon the sale of an individual shareholder's stock to an S corporation ESOP, he or she will not qualify for the tax-deferred "rollover" that is available to individual shareholders of a C corporation;[17]

- The increased limits for tax deductions for contributions to a leveraged ESOP, when used to pay interest on an exempt loan to the plan, are not available for S corporations;[18] and

- S corporations are not entitled to deduct cash dividends paid on stock held by an ESOP that are used to pay principal or interest on a loan used to acquire the stock or that are passed through to plan participants.[19]

No Section 1042 Tax-Deferred Sales

A tax incentive that has spurred great interest in ESOPs for closely held companies is the opportunity provided under Section 1042 of the Code for a tax-free "rollover" of the proceeds of a sale of stock by a shareholder to an ESOP if the proceeds are reinvested in securities of other corporations.[20] This special tax treatment is available only with sales of stock of closely held C corporations.[21]

However, as of this writing (fall 2014), there are pending before the Senate and the House of Representatives parallel bills that look to extend Code Section 1042 treatment to S corporations, among other things.[22] If passed, the bills would: (1) amend Code Section 1042 to allow an S corporation shareholder to defer recognition of capital gain realized

---

17. Code § 1042(c)(1)(A).

18. Code § 404(a)(9)(c).

19. Code § 404(k)(1).

20. Code § 1042(a).

21. Code § 1042(c)(1)(A).

22. See H.R. 4837: Promotion and Expansion of Private Employee Ownership Act of 2014 and S. 742: Promotion and Expansion of Private Employee Ownership Act of 2014.

from the sale of employer securities to an ESOP; (2) add a new section to the Code permitting banks to deduct 50% of the interest received from a qualified securities acquisition loan; (3) add a new section to the Code requiring the Secretary of the Treasury to establish the "S Corporation Employee Ownership Assistance Office" to foster employee ownership of S corporations; and (4) amend the Small Business Act to permit a corporation eligible to participate in loan, contracting assistance, or business development programs to remain eligible to participate after an ESOP acquires 50% or more of the corporation.

Limit on Contributions

The maximum amount that a corporation may deduct for contributions to an ESOP generally is 25% of the compensation paid to all employees participating in the plan for the taxable year.[23] However, increased limits for employer contributions are available for amounts allocated to repay an ESOP loan incurred to finance the purchase of employer stock. Contributions by a C corporation used to pay interest on this kind of loan are fully deductible in addition to contributions used to pay the principal amount of an ESOP loan, which are deductible up to 25% of the compensation of the participating employees.[24] However,

---

23. Code § 404(a)(3)(A).

24. Code § 404(a)(9). This amount is deductible *in addition to* contributions used for other purposes, which are deductible up to 25% of covered compensation. See PLR 200732028. In PLR 200732028, the taxpayer described a plan that had a leveraged ESOP component and another plan component, and the taxpayer stated that it would amend the plan to clarify that the plan's trust would be prohibited from applying contributions that the taxpayer intends to deduct under Section 404(a)(3) of the Code to payments of principal and interest on the plan's acquisition loans. Based on the taxpayer's representations, the IRS concluded that the taxpayer could deduct the contributions to the plan for general purposes under Section 404(a)(3) of the Code and separately deduct the contributions to the plan for repayment of acquisition loans under Section 404(a)(9) of the Code in the same taxable year and subject to separate limitations. In other words, this PLR removed the requirement that a corporation sponsor an ESOP and a separate other plan to maximize the limits of deductible contributions to 50%: now, so long as the plan has a leveraged ESOP component and a separate component (profit sharing or stock bonus portion that is not a leveraged ESOP), a corporation may claim

..outions by an S corporation used to pay interest on an ESOP loan will count against the 25% limit.[25]

No Deduction for Dividends

Dividends paid on shares held by a C corporation ESOP may be deducted under the following circumstances: (1) if they are paid in cash to plan participants; (2) if they are paid to the plan and passed through to the participants within 90 days after the end of the plan year; (3) if they are used to repay a loan incurred to purchase the company stock on which the dividends are paid; or (4) if they are paid to the plan and, at the election of the plan participants, are reinvested in employer securities.[26] However, this deduction for dividends on stock held by an ESOP is not available for S corporations.[27] Where an S corporation ESOP owns all of the outstanding shares of the corporation, the fact that dividends are not deductible will not have any effect because the corporation's income will not be subject to tax, either at the corporate or at the shareholder level.[28] However, in the situation where an ESOP owns less than all of the outstanding shares of the plan sponsor, the failure of Congress to extend the dividends-paid deduction to S corporation ESOPs may result in greater taxable income for the other shareholders than would be the case with a C corporation declaring the same amount of dividends.

Unresolved Issues

Distributions of S Corporation Earnings to Plan Participants

Excise Tax on Premature Distributions. One area of ambiguity regarding the rules for S corporation ESOPs relates to how distributions of S corporation earnings to ESOP participants should be treated. Distri-

---

a separate deduction for contributions to each component of the plan. Of course, the contributions to such plan remain subject to all other applicable laws and regulations, including Section 415 of the Code.

25. Code § 404(a)(9)(C).
26. Code § 404(k).
27. Code § 404(k)(1).
28. Code §§ 1363(a) and 501(a).

butions received from a tax-qualified plan by a participant before he or she has attained age 59½ are subject to a 10% excise tax.[29] This tax does not apply to "dividends" on stock of a C corporation as described in Section 404(k) of the Code.[30] Section 404(k) of the Code provides, as a general rule, that in the case of a C corporation, there will be allowed as a deduction the amount of any dividend paid on shares held by an ESOP if the dividend is paid in cash to the participants in the plan, is used to make payments on an ESOP loan, or is reinvested in employer securities.[31] Because distributions by S corporations technically do not constitute "dividends" within the meaning of the Code,[32] the question arises whether the pass-through of S corporation earnings to ESOP plan participants should be treated in the same manner as dividends declared by a C corporation that are passed through to ESOP participants, or whether the excise tax on premature distributions should apply.

---

29. Code § 72(t).

30. Code § 72(t)(2)(A)(vi).

31. Code § 404(k)(2).

32. The term "dividend" is defined in Section 316 of the Code to mean any distribution of property made by a corporation to its shareholders out of its current or accumulated "earnings and profits." In the case of a C corporation, a distribution that is a dividend is included in the gross income of the shareholders to whom the dividend is paid. Code § 301(c). Different rules are provided for distributions of property made by S corporations with respect to their stock. If an S corporation has no earnings and profits from years during which it was a C corporation, distributions then generally will be tax-free to the extent of the shareholders' bases in their stock. Code § 1368(b). An S corporation shareholder will be subject to tax on any distribution to the extent that it exceeds his or her stock basis. Code § 1368(b)(2). If a C corporation converts to S corporation status at a time when it has accumulated earnings and profits, then distributions will remain tax-free up to the amount of the corporation's "accumulated adjustments account," which is an account consisting of the corporation's net undistributed income accumulated after 1982. Code § 1368(c). If a distribution exceeds the accumulated adjustments account, the excess amount is treated as a dividend to the extent of the corporation's accumulated earnings and profits. Code § 1368(c)(2). In other words, a distribution by an S corporation with respect to its stock is not a "dividend" for tax purposes unless the amount of the distribution exceeds the corporation's accumulated adjustments account and the corporation has accumulated earnings and profits.

Small Cash-Outs. A related issue is whether the consent of the ESOP participants must be obtained before distributions from an S corporation to an ESOP may be passed through to the participants. No accrued benefit under an employee benefit plan with a present value in excess of $1,000 may be immediately distributed to a participant in a tax-qualified employee benefit plan without his or her consent.[33] This provision does not apply to a distribution of dividends from an ESOP to which Section 404(k) of the Code applies.[34] Because the exception applies only to "dividends," it could be argued that the general rule requiring employee consent to distributions applies to all distributions from an S corporation ESOP, including distributions of the S corporation's earnings. It is not clear whether Congress intended that different rules would apply with regard to distributions of C corporation and S corporation earnings.

IRA Rollovers

Another issue relating to distributions of S corporation earnings to ESOP participants is whether these distributions are eligible for a tax-free rollover into an individual retirement arrangement (an "IRA") or into another tax-qualified plan. The regulations exclude from the definition of an "eligible rollover distribution" dividends paid on employer securities as described in Section 404(k) of the Code.[35] Before the enactment of the American Jobs Creation Act of 2004, the IRS had taken the position that distributions by an S corporation on stock that is not pledged as collateral to secure an ESOP loan could not be used to pay off that loan because those distributions are not "dividends" within the meaning of Section 404(k) of the Code.[36] By this reasoning, it would seem to follow that S corporation distributions should not be treated as dividends that are not eligible for a tax-free rollover.[37]

---

33. Code § 411(a)(11).

34. Code § 404(k)(1).

35. Treas. Regs. § 1.402(c)-2, Q&A 4(e).

36. PLR 199938052 (July 2, 1999). The American Jobs Creation Act of 2004 contained a provision authorizing the use by an ESOP of distributions on S corporation stock that has not been pledged as collateral to secure an ESOP loan to pay off that loan. P.L. 108-357, 118 Stat. 1418, §240(a).

37. The author is aware that representatives of the national office of the IRS have informally expressed the view that distributions of S corporation earnings

Delayed Distribution of Leveraged Shares

Section 409(o)(1)(B) of the Code generally permits an ESOP to defer the commencement of distributions of shares acquired with a "loan described in Section 404(a)(9)" until the complete repayment of that loan. Section 404(a)(9) provides that, notwithstanding the general limitations on the amounts that may be contributed to defined contribution pension plans, contributions made to an ESOP and applied by the plan to the repayment of the principal of a loan incurred for the purpose of acquiring qualifying employer securities are deductible up to 25% of the compensation otherwise paid or accrued during the taxable year to the employees under the ESOP.[38] It is unclear whether a loan to an S corporation ESOP is "described in Section 404(a)(9)" for this purpose, because Section 404(a)(9)(c) provides that "[t]his paragraph shall not apply to an S corporation." IRS representatives have informally indicated that Section 409(o)(1)(B) is not applicable to an S corporation ESOP, but the author is aware that a number of favorable determination letters have been issued for S corporation ESOPs incorporating the deferral of distributions permitted by this section of the Code.

Planning Opportunities

Income Tax Deferral

Significant tax savings opportunities are available for ESOP companies that make the S election. This can be illustrated most dramatically by considering a corporation in which an ESOP owns all of the stock. If that corporation makes the S election, there will be no current federal tax on its annual income. The corporation will not be subject to tax under the general S corporation rules,[39] and, although the income will be passed through to its sole shareholder (the ESOP), no shareholder-

---

are not "dividends" within the meaning of Section 316 of the Code and that, therefore: (1) S corporation distributions are subject to the 10% excise tax on premature distributions if they are passed through to participants in an ESOP; (2) the consent of an ESOP participant must be obtained before a distribution from an S corporation to an ESOP may be passed through to him or her; and (3) S corporation distributions are eligible for a tax-free rollover into an IRA.

38. Code § 404(a)(9)(C).

39. Code § 1363(a).

level tax will be imposed because the ESOP is a tax-exempt entity.[40] In effect, the income tax will be deferred until the participants in the ESOP receive their benefits (which will most likely be much larger than they would have been if the ESOP trust had been taxed on its share of the S corporation earnings). It should also be noted that participants may further defer their tax liability by rolling their benefits over into IRAs.[41] However, as discussed below, certain additional taxes are imposed on S corporations and participants in S corporation ESOPs where the benefits under an ESOP are allocated primarily to a small group of employees or where the corporation has issued large and concentrated amounts of synthetic equity.

Where an ESOP company has shareholders in addition to the ESOP, tax savings still will be available by making the S election, but the S election may not have a positive impact on the corporation's cash flow. This is because, in most cases, S corporation shareholders must withdraw sufficient funds to cover payment of their taxes on the corporation's income. If tax distributions are required to be made to the shareholders other than the ESOP, an equivalent distribution also will have to be made to the ESOP, even though it will incur no tax liability, because otherwise the economic rights associated with the ESOP's shares will be different from those associated with the other shares. This, of course, would violate the one-class-of-stock rule for S corporations and result in termination of the S election.[42] The potential impact of the S election on an ESOP company's cash flow can be illustrated by the following example:

> *Example 1.* Assume that an S corporation sponsors an ESOP that owns 30% of its outstanding shares and that its taxable income for 2014 is $1 million. There will be allocated to the shareholders other than the ESOP $700,000 of the corporation's income, upon which they will incur a federal tax liability of approximately $245,000.[43] If the corporation distributes $245,000 to the other shareholders, it will be required to distribute an equivalent amount, or $105,000, to the ESOP. After the distributions, the S corporation will have

---

40. Code §§ 401(a), 501(a), and 512(e)(3).

41. Code § 402(c).

42. Code § 1361(b)(1)(D).

43. This calculation assumes that the shareholders are in the maximum individual tax bracket of 35%. Code § 1.

retained earnings of $650,000. If the corporation were a C corporation, its corporate tax liability would be $350,000,[44] and the corporation would be able to retain $650,000 after taxes (assuming no dividends are declared), or as much as in the S corporation case.

This example illustrates that the S election may not be advantageous for a rapidly growing ESOP company that needs to retain earnings to fund future expansion (unless all of the company's shares are held by the ESOP). On the other hand, the S election still might be advantageous under various other circumstances. For example, the S election would be advantageous where the corporation could declare dividends in an amount in excess of the shareholders' tax liability because it did not need to retain most of its earnings. The S election also would be advantageous if the cash distributed to the ESOP could be used to fund other corporate obligations. This might be the case where the cash distributed to the ESOP could be used to fund the corporation's repurchase obligation.[45] The S election also might be advantageous where the cash distributed to the ESOP could be used to buy more shares from the plan sponsor, which then could use the sale proceeds to provide funds for other business needs. This would require the approval of the ESOP trustee or other fiduciary, who would have to determine that the proposed use of the cash is in the best interest of the participants in the plan.[46]

Another situation where the S election would be advantageous would be where the individual shareholders are willing to pay the tax on their share of the corporation's income out of their own personal funds. This might be feasible in a situation where the ESOP owns most, but not all, of the outstanding shares. If the individual shareholders have substantial personal wealth in addition to their company stock, or if they are employed by the corporation and their compensation can be

---

44. This calculation assumes that the corporation is subject to tax at the rate of 35% of its taxable income. Code § 11(b).

45. Until 2004, there was some ambiguity regarding whether S corporation distributions on allocated ESOP shares could be used to pay down an ESOP loan. As discussed at footnote 36, the IRS had taken the position that this could not be done, PLR 199938052 (July 2, 1999), but the Code was amended in 2004 to specifically allow S corporation distributions to be so used. American Jobs Creation of 2004, P.L. 108-357, 118 Stat. 1418, § 240(a).

46. ERISA § 404(a)(1)(A).

increased to an amount where they are willing to pay the tax on their share of the S corporation's earnings out of their own funds, it may be possible for the corporation to avoid the payment of dividends.

Should ESOP Companies Make the S Election?

Income Tax Deferral

The question whether existing ESOP companies should make the S election can be determined only on a case-by-case basis, depending on each company's particular facts and circumstances. In some cases, the opportunity for the tax deferral described above will be appealing. However, because most individual S corporation shareholders require distributions to cover the taxes on their share of the corporation's income, the ESOP companies that will derive a significant benefit from the tax-deferral opportunity may be limited to those companies where the ESOP owns all or substantially all of the outstanding shares.

Tax-Deferred Sales to ESOPs

The failure of Congress to extend to S corporations all of the ESOP tax incentives that are available to C corporations also will limit the number of ESOP companies that make the S election. Most importantly, where individual shareholders of an ESOP company are planning to arrange tax-deferred sales of some or all of their shares to the ESOP in the future, the S election will be unattractive. However, it may be possible for a shareholder who desires to arrange for a tax-deferred sale to an ESOP to obtain the best of both worlds by arranging for the sale to close in a year when the plan sponsor is a C corporation and for the S election to be made effective for a later year. A problem will remain for business owners who desire to arrange for two- or three-stage ESOP buyouts. If an S election is made after the first ESOP sale, subsequent sales of stock to the ESOP will not qualify for the tax deferral unless the S election is first terminated. Once an S election is terminated, it cannot be reinstated for five years.[47]

---

47. Code § 1362(g). The IRS has stated that it will not exercise its authority to waive this rule when a 50% ownership change has occurred if that ownership

In some cases, shareholders of S corporations have built up significant tax bases in the shares of their S corporations, and sales of their shares to an ESOP might be attractive even without the opportunity for a deferral of the capital gains tax. An S corporation shareholder's basis in his or her shares is increased by his or her share of the corporation's income and is reduced by distributions.[48] To the extent that an S corporation has retained earnings, the shareholders will have increased tax bases in their shares. Another situation in which an S corporation shareholder may have a high stock basis is where the stock has recently been inherited. In that case, the shareholder's basis is equal to the fair market value as of the date of the decedent's death.[49] Where an S corporation shareholder has a high basis in his or her shares, the shares can be sold at a reduced capital gain. The less the amount of the gain, the less important the tax-deferral election becomes. The importance of the tax-deferral election also is lessened when capital gains tax rates are relatively low, as had been the case during the first decade of the 21st century. However, the current tax rate that selling shareholders face is as high as 23.8%, a 60% increase since 2012. This reflects an increase from a 15% to a 20% federal capital gains tax rate under the American Taxpayer Relief Act of 2012 for those in the highest tax bracket. In addition, the Health Care and Education Reconciliation Act of 2010 added a new 3.8% Medicare surtax on "net investment income." This 3.8% Medicare surtax applies to taxpayers with "net investment income" who exceed threshold income amounts of $200,000 for single filers and $250,000 for married couples filing jointly. Pursuant to Code Section 1411, "net investment income" includes interest, dividends, capital gains, retirement income, and income from partnerships (as well as other forms of "unearned income").

Limits on Plan Contributions

The attractiveness of the S election for an ESOP company also may be reduced by the fact that the limit on the amount that can be contributed

---

change arises in connection with a sale of stock to an ESOP that qualifies for nonrecognition of gain under Section 1042 of the Code. PLR 199952072 (Sept. 27, 1999).

48. Code § 1367(a).

49. Code § 1014.

to a leveraged ESOP by an S corporation is lower than the amount that can be contributed by a C corporation. The limit on tax-deductible contributions is 25% of covered compensation, but in the case of an S corporation, contributions applied to pay interest on an ESOP loan count against the limit,[50] while contributions to an ESOP by a C corporation for this purpose do not count against the limit.[51] However, in most cases where the annual payments due under the ESOP loan exceed the maximum amount that can be contributed to the ESOP on a tax-deductible basis, it will be possible to cover the shortfall with S corporation distributions.

Another strategy for dealing with the lower contribution limits available for S corporation ESOPs is simply to extend the term of the ESOP loan to the point where the annual contribution required to service the debt falls within the 25% limit. This can be accomplished under a "back-to-back" loan structure, pursuant to which the plan sponsor borrows funds from an outside lender on normal commercial terms (with, for example, a seven-year amortization period), and the plan sponsor then loans the borrowed funds to the ESOP on extended payment terms (for example, a 15-year amortization period). No prepayment penalty should be provided for in the loan agreement between the plan sponsor and the ESOP, so that if the plan sponsor's covered payroll increases, the ESOP loan can be repaid more rapidly. The interest rate on the ESOP loan could be set at the minimum rate required to avoid triggering imputed interest, regardless of the interest payable to the outside lender, which will minimize the effect of the requirement that interest payments on an ESOP loan for an S corporation must be counted against the 25% limit.

Corporate-Level Tax

Another factor that an ESOP company should take into account in determining whether to make the S election is whether the election may trigger unanticipated corporate-level taxation. Although as a general rule S corporations are not subject to tax, there are three exceptions. First, an S corporation that formerly was a C corporation is subject to

---

50.   Code § 404(a)(9)(C).

51.   Code § 404(a)(9)(B).

tax on "built-in" gains recognized within 10 years of the effective date of the S election.[52] As discussed below, "built-in" gains are gains that are attributable to the period before the effective date of the S election.[53] If an ESOP company anticipates selling its assets or liquidating within 10 years from the date of the S election, the built-in gain tax may substantially diminish the benefits of the S election.

A second corporate-level tax to which an S corporation may be subjected is a LIFO "recapture" tax. When a C corporation which uses the LIFO inventory method makes the S election, it must include as income, over a four-year period, the excess of the value of its inventory determined on a FIFO basis over its value determined on a LIFO basis.[54] Finally, a corporation that makes the S election may be subject to tax on "excess net passive income."[55] ESOP companies that derive substantial amounts of their income from passive sources, such as rents, royalties, dividends, and interest, should evaluate the possible imposition of this tax before making the S election.

Compliance with Anti-Abuse Rules

An S corporation sponsoring an ESOP is required to comply with special anti-abuse rules discussed below. Failure to plan for and comply with these anti-abuse rules can result in the imposition of draconian taxes and penalties.

The 100% ESOP-Owned S Corporation

As discussed above, the tax savings and corporate cash-flow enhancements that can be obtained by an ESOP company that makes the S election are maximized when the ESOP owns all of the outstanding stock of the corporation. For this reason, many ESOP companies have arranged for the buyout of all of their shareholders other than the ESOP, and a number of companies that have adopted ESOPs in recent years have

---

52. Code § 1374.
53. Code § 1374(d).
54. Code § 1363(d).
55. Code § 1375.

arranged for the ESOP to obtain 100% ownership in one transaction. Complex financing arrangements are necessary to arrange for a 100% or near-100% ESOP buyout of a company, and once an S corporation becomes 100% ESOP-owned, it generally is necessary to develop equity incentive compensation arrangements for management other than traditional stock options and stock-based plans.

Financing the 100% ESOP Transaction

The majority of the funding for a 100% ESOP buyout of a company typically is comprised of a senior credit facility provided by one or more banks or other institutional lenders. The remainder of the financing typically is obtained from one or more of the following sources: institutional subordinated or "mezzanine" lenders; the selling shareholders; a private equity firm or other source of equity capital; or the employees themselves, via transfers of funds from other tax-qualified employee benefit plans. Where either mezzanine lending or seller financing is involved in a transaction, it typically is necessary for the borrower to pay a higher rate of interest on the subordinated loan than on the senior indebtedness, reflecting the greater risk being assumed by the subordinated lender; and it also often is necessary to enhance the rate of return for the subordinated lender with an equity "kicker." Typically, the equity kicker takes the form of options to purchase stock of the borrower. These types of options generally are referred to as warrants. Where the borrower is an S corporation, it is important to assure that warrants issued to subordinated lenders will not be treated as stock for federal income tax purposes. If the warrants are treated as stock, the company's S election will be terminated by reason of violation of the one-class-of-stock requirement because the warrants will have rights and preferences different from the rights and preferences associated with the common stock.

Fortunately, warrants issued by S corporations to lenders generally will not be treated as a second class of stock. The regulations provide that an option will not be treated as a second class of stock if it is issued to a person who is "actively and regularly engaged in the business of lending" and if the option is issued "in connection with a commercially reasonable loan to the corporation."[56] If seller financing is involved in

---

56.   Treas. Regs. § 1.1361-1(l)(4)(iii)(B)(1).

an ESOP transaction, the following two conditions must be satisfied for any warrants issued to the sellers not to be treated as a second class of stock: (1) the warrants must not be "substantially certain to be exercised," and (2) the strike price for the warrants must not be substantially below the fair market value of the underlying stock on the date that the option is issued (or on the date that the warrants are transferred to a person who is not eligible to hold shares of an S corporation or the date upon which the warrants are "materially modified").[57]

In addition to the rules described above for determining whether a stock option or warrant issued by an S corporation will be treated as a second class of stock, there is a safe-harbor rule under which an option will not be treated as a second class of stock if, on the date that the option is issued, the strike price is at least 90% of the fair market value of the underlying stock.[58] The regulations provide that a good-faith determination of fair market value by the corporation will be respected "unless it can be shown that the value was substantially in error and the determination of the value was not performed with reasonable diligence to obtain a fair value."[59]

Even where some of the funding for a 100% ESOP buyout will be provided by a private equity firm or other equity source, it will be in the interest of all of the parties to structure the financing in the form of subordinated debt with warrants attached. As long as the warrants are properly structured so as to avoid being treated as a second class of stock, the corporation then will retain its eligibility to make the S election and will not be required to make any earnings distributions to cover shareholder-level taxes.

Where some of the funding for an ESOP transaction will be provided by the employees by means of transfers from other tax-qualified

---

57. Treas. Regs. § 1.1361-1(l)(4)(iii)(A). If an option is issued in connection with a loan and the time period during which the option can be exercised is extended in connection with (and consistent with) a modification of the terms of the loan, then the extension of the time period during which the option may be exercised will not be considered to be a material modification.

58. Treas. Regs. § 1.1361-1(l)(4)(iii)(C).

59. Ibid. Failure of an option to satisfy these safe-harbor standards will not necessarily result in the option being treated as a second class of stock. Rather, the holder of the option simply will not be entitled to the presumption that the option is not stock provided by the safe-harbor rule.

plans, there will be no need to provide equity "enhancements," through the use of warrants or otherwise, because the employees will be able to hold equity interests through the ESOP. The funds that they invest in the transaction typically are transferred to the ESOP from a profit-sharing or Section 401(k) plan sponsored by the ESOP company. Although the employees' interests will be equity interests, these interests will not be a second class of stock. Rather, there will be allocated to their accounts stock of the same class as the other stock held by the ESOP. If an ESOP transaction is funded in part with transfers to the ESOP of account balances from other employee benefit plans, care must be taken to assure compliance with all applicable federal and state securities laws.[60]

Equity Incentives for Employees

Equity compensation arrangements for executives of 100% ESOP-owned S corporations generally must be designed in a way that does not involve actual grants of stock. If any of the executives become stockholders, they will be required to report a proportionate amount of the company's earnings on their personal income tax returns. In turn, this likely would require the corporation to distribute to the executives earnings in an amount sufficient to cover the taxes on their shares of the company's income, and the company then would be required to make proportionate distributions to the ESOP, as discussed above. The tax savings from the S election then would not result in enhanced cash flows to the company. Therefore, incentive compensation arrangements for executives of ESOP-owned S corporations generally take the form of stock options,[61] phantom stock, or stock appreciation rights.

---

60. For a discussion of the applicable federal and state securities law, see Maldonado, 362-3d T.M., *Securities Law Aspects of Employee Benefit Plans*.

61. Of course, once any of the options are exercised, the persons acquiring stock will become subject to tax on their share of the S corporation's income. This will raise the tax-distributions problem discussed above. Therefore, stock option plans for employees of a 100% ESOP-owned corporation generally are structured in a way to provide for a cash-out of the options at their time of exercise. Similar arrangements typically are made for warrants issued to subordinated lenders who provide financing for 100% ESOP-owned companies.

Compensation planning for executives is further complicated in an ESOP-owned company because equity incentive arrangements, like warrants granted to subordinated lenders, must be carefully structured to avoid being treated as a second class of stock. Options granted by an S corporation to employees in connection with the performance of services will not be treated as a second class of stock if the following conditions are satisfied: (1) they are not excessive in comparison to the value of the services performed; (2) they are nontransferrable; and (3) they do not have a "readily ascertainable fair market value" at the time that they are issued.[62] Options issued by S corporations almost never will have a "readily ascertainable fair market value." Therefore, compliance with the one-class-of-stock rule in connection with the issuance by an S corporation of stock options generally can be assured by making the options nontransferrable.[63]

In addition to stock options, ESOP-owned S corporations also often use phantom stock or stock appreciation rights to compensate key executives. These types of so-called "synthetic equity" arrangements generally will not be treated as a second class of stock for federal income tax purposes. However, the use of these types of arrangements by ESOP-owned S corporations is limited by the anti-abuse rules described below.

Anti-Abuse Rules for S Corporation ESOPs

Perceived Abuses

Shortly after S corporations first became eligible to sponsor ESOPs in 1998, two abuses arose. The first abuse involved the adoption of ESOPs by S corporations that had only one or a few employees. For example, a highly paid professional might seek to defer taxes indefinitely by incorporating his or her business and then transferring all of the stock of the corporation to an ESOP. The professional person would be the sole participant in the ESOP, and the sole purpose for setting up the ESOP would be to defer tax on the income generated from the professional's business activities. This use of an ESOP obviously does not serve the

---

62. Treas. Regs. § 1.1361-1(l)(4)(iii)(B)(2).

63. For a discussion of the tax treatment of stock options granted by S corporations, see David Ackerman, "Stock Options for S Corporations," *Journal of Employee Ownership Law and Finance* 13, no. 3 (summer 2001): 55.

policy underlying ESOP legislation, which is to promote broad-based employee ownership and thereby enhance employee productivity.

A second abuse of the use of ESOPs by S corporations involved a so-called "tax holiday" for newly formed enterprises, where executives and outside investors held stock options and other forms of equity interests which, over time, would substantially dilute the ESOP's ownership. The equity interests for the executives and outside investors could be designed in such a way as to defer their recognition of income over a period of several years, during which time all of the corporate earnings would be reported by the ESOP and thereby escape taxation (the "tax holiday"). If the ESOP will be substantially diluted after the stock options are exercised and the other equity interests vest, the ESOP will have served only to avoid taxes and not to promote employee ownership.[64]

To eliminate the two abuses described above and any similar tax avoidance schemes, Congress enacted a set of special anti-abuse rules for S corporation ESOPs, which are set forth in Section 409(p) of the Code. Under Section 409(p), an ESOP that holds shares of an S corporation is prohibited from allocating employer securities to certain persons who are identified as "disqualified persons" during any "nonallocation year."[65] The term "nonallocation year" means a year in which disqualified persons own at least 50% of the outstanding shares of the plan sponsor.[66]

Disqualified Persons

For purposes of Section 409(p), a person is a "disqualified person" if either (1) he or she is deemed to own 10% or more of the "deemed-owned shares" of the corporation, or (2) the aggregate number of shares deemed to be owned by the person, together with the shares deemed to be owned by members of his or her family, is at least 20% of the total deemed-owned shares of the corporation.[67] A participant in

---

64. For an example of how an abusive "tax holiday" transaction might have been structured, see Ginsburg, "The Taxpayer Relief Act of 1997: Worse Than You Think," *Tax Notes* 76 (Sept. 29, 1997): 1790.

65. Code § 409(p)(1).

66. Code § 409(p)(3).

67. Code § 409(p)(4). The definition of "member of the family," for purposes of Code Section 409(p)(4), is set forth in Code Section 409(p)(4)(D) and means,

an S corporation ESOP is deemed to own shares that are allocated to his or her ESOP account and a portion of the shares which are held in the suspense account and that have not been allocated to participants' accounts.[68] A participant's share of unallocated stock is the amount of that stock that would be allocated to him or her if the unallocated stock were allocated to all participants in the plan in the same proportion as the most recent stock allocation under the plan.[69]

In addition, an individual who owns "synthetic equity" in an S corporation will be deemed to own the shares of stock on which the synthetic equity is based if this will result in the treatment of him or her as a disqualified person.[70] The term "synthetic equity" is defined to mean any stock option, warrant, restricted stock, deferred issuance stock right, or similar interest or right that gives the holder the right to acquire or receive stock of the S corporation in the future.[71] The term "synthetic equity" also includes stock appreciation rights, phantom stock units, and similar rights to future cash payments based on the value of stock or growth in the value of stock.[72]

In determining whether an individual is a "disqualified person," only shares held for the benefit of the individual through the ESOP or

---

with respect to an individual: (1) the spouse of the individual; (2) an ancestor or lineal descendant of the individual or the individual's spouse; (3) a brother or sister of the individual or of the individual's spouse and any lineal descendant of the brother or sister; and (4) the spouse of any individual described in paragraph (2) or (3).

68. Code § 409(p)(4)(C)(i).

69. Code § 409(p)(4)(C)(ii).

70. Code § 409(p)(5). The regulations interpreting Section 409(p) of the Code make it clear that the determination of whether someone is a disqualified person is made by way of a two-step analysis: first without regard to any synthetic equity attributable to that person and, second, by taking synthetic equity into account. Treas. Reg. § 1.409(p)-1(d)(1).

71. Code § 409(p)(6)(C). In Revenue Ruling 2004-4 (2004-6 I.R.B.), the IRS held that rights to acquire stock in entities related to the plan sponsor also could be treated as synthetic equity. The ruling set forth three different situations involving S corporation ESOPs in which subsidiary stock options were used to enable certain individuals to obtain tax benefits associated with S corporation status, while severely limiting the ESOP's ability to benefit from the company's profits.

72. Ibid. See also Treas. Reg. § 1.409(p)-1(f)(2)(ii).

on which synthetic equity is based count as "deemed-owned shares." Shares held outright by an individual, outside of the ESOP, are *not* "deemed-owned shares."

> *Example 2.* Corporation X is an S corporation. It has 10,000 shares outstanding, 7,000 of which are held by an ESOP. Arthur is a participant in the ESOP, and 600 shares are allocated to his ESOP account. Arthur's nephew, Bob, also is a participant in the ESOP, and 450 shares are allocated to his ESOP account. In addition, Bob owns 2,000 shares of X outside the ESOP. There are 4,000 shares of X remaining in the ESOP loan suspense account. Last year, 5% of the total shares released from the suspense account were allocated to Arthur's company stock account, and 3% of the total shares released from the suspense account were allocated to Bob's company stock account. Arthur is deemed to own 800 shares—the 600 shares allocated to his company stock account, plus 200 of the suspense account shares (4,000 x 5%). Arthur is a disqualified person, because his 800 deemed-owned shares constitute more than 10% of the total of 7,000 (700) deemed-owned shares. Bob, however, is not a disqualified person, because he is deemed to own only 570 shares—the 450 shares allocated to his company stock account, plus 120 of the suspense account shares (400 x 3%). Application of the family aggregation rules to Bob does not result in his becoming a disqualified person, because the total number of the deemed-owned shares held by Arthur (800) plus Bob (570) is less than 20% of the 7,000 (1,400) total deemed-owned shares. The 200 shares that Bob owns outside the ESOP are not counted in calculating the number of shares that he is deemed to own.[73]

> *Example 3.* Corporation Y is an S corporation. It has 10,000 shares outstanding, all of which are held by an ESOP and are allocated to the accounts of the participants in the plan. Cindy and Debbie are participants in the plan. Cindy has 625 shares allocated to her ESOP account, and Debbie has 1,000 shares allocated to her account. Cindy has an option to purchase 1,000 shares of Y's stock. In determining whether Cindy is a disqualified person, she is deemed to own both the 625 shares allocated to her ESOP account plus the 1,000 shares covered by her option. In determining the percentage of her ownership of the deemed-owned shares, the denominator of her fractional interest is 11,000 (the 10,000 outstanding shares held by the ESOP, plus the 1,000 shares covered by Cindy's option). Cindy's ownership is 14.8% (1,625 ÷ 11,000), which makes Cindy a disqualified person. Debbie also is a disqualified person because she is deemed to own 1,000 of 10,000 deemed-owned shares, which is 10% of the total deemed-owned shares. The 1,000 shares covered by Cindy's option are

---

73. Examples 2 through 7 are based on examples that were developed by Luis Granados, whose assistance in the preparation of this chapter is gratefully acknowledged.

not taken into account in determining the percentage of deemed owned shares held by Debbie.[74] For purposes of determining whether there is a nonallocation year, both Cindy's and Debbie's shares will be included in the computation.

Nonallocation Year

If an S corporation sponsors an ESOP and any of the participants in the ESOP or any holders of synthetic equity are "disqualified persons," and if these disqualified persons own at least 50% of the outstanding shares of the corporation, then there will be a nonallocation year, and the penalty taxes set forth in Section 409(p) of the Code will be triggered.[75] In determining whether the disqualified persons own 50% or more of the outstanding shares, there must be counted not only the shares actually owned by the disqualified persons, but also their "deemed-owned" shares plus shares that they are considered to own for federal income tax purposes under attribution-of-ownership rules.[76] Under these rules, an individual is considered as owning stock that is held by his or her spouse and by his or her children, grandchildren, and parents.[77] Moreover, for purposes of Section 409(p), an individual also will be considered to own shares held by any of his or her brothers or sisters, or brothers-in-law or sisters-in-law, or by any children or grandchildren of any brother or sister or brother-in-law or sister-in-law.[78] Individuals also are considered to own shares that are held in partnerships, estates, trusts, and corporations that they control.[79]

Putting all these rules together, in order to determine whether an S corporation is subject to Section 409(p), the holdings of equity interests in the company should be analyzed as follows:

1. *Step One:* determine whether any of the participants in the ESOP or any of the holders of synthetic equity are disqualified persons:

---

74. Treas. Reg. § 1.409(p)-1(d)(1)(ii).
75. Code § 409(p)(3)(A).
76. Code § 409(p)(3)(B).
77. Code § 318(a).
78. Code §§ 409(p)(3)(B)(i)(I), 409(p)(4)(D).
79. Code § 318(a).

    a. determine whether any participants in the ESOP or any of the holders of synthetic equity will be deemed to own at least 10% of the total number of deemed-owned shares; and

    b. determine whether any of the participants in the ESOP or any of the holders of synthetic equity are disqualified persons by reason of aggregate deemed ownership by the participant or synthetic equity holder and by members of his or her family of at least 20% of the total number of deemed-owned shares.

2. *Step Two:* determine the aggregate amount of shares owned or deemed to be owned by all of the disqualified persons, taking into account both the attribution-of-ownership rules and the synthetic-equity rules.

The second step of the analysis must be applied twice—once without taking synthetic equity into account and once with synthetic equity taken into account. First, if the number of the outstanding shares of the company owned or deemed to be owned by the disqualified persons (excluding all synthetic equity) is at least 50% of the corporation's total outstanding shares at any time during any plan year, then that year is a nonallocation year. Second, if the disqualified persons own or are deemed to own (including their synthetic equity share equivalents) at least 50% of the total outstanding shares plus the total synthetic equity share equivalents held by disqualified persons (but excluding synthetic equity share equivalents held by other persons), then the year will be a nonallocation year.[80]

> *Example 4.* Corporation Z is an S corporation, and it has 1,000 shares outstanding, all of which are held by an ESOP. Ellen has an option to acquire 1,050 shares, and Frank has an option to acquire 100 shares. Neither Ellen nor Frank are participants in the ESOP, and they are not related to each other or to any of the ESOP participants. No ESOP participant has a large enough allocation to be a disqualified person. Ellen is a disqualified person because she owns more than 10% of the deemed-owned shares through her synthetic equity.[81] Frank is not a disqualified person because he owns less than 10%

---

80. Treas. Reg. § 1.409(p)-1(c)(1)(ii)(B).

81. The shares covered by Frank's option cannot be counted in determining whether Ellen is a disqualified person. Only Ellen's synthetic equity can be counted for this purpose. Treas. Reg. § 1.409(p)-1(d)(1)(ii).

of the deemed-owned shares. The company passes the first test for avoiding a nonallocation year because the only disqualified person (Ellen) owns less than 50% of the outstanding shares—she owns none of them. The company fails the second test, however, because Ellen owns more than 50% of the sum of the total of outstanding shares plus shares of synthetic equity held by disqualified persons—1,050 out of a total of 2,050 shares. If the shares covered by Frank's option could be counted, then there would not be a nonallocation year, because Ellen would own 1,050 out of 2,150 total shares. However, the regulations clearly provide that synthetic equity held by persons who are not disqualified persons is excluded from the computation.[82]

Synthetic Equity

Buy-Sell Agreements

The treatment of synthetic equity has been a source of confusion under Section 409(p). Problems of interpretation are presented by the broad definition of the term "synthetic equity." The statute provides that this term includes *any* option or right to acquire shares, not merely the right to acquire newly issued shares.[83] Therefore, the law might be interpreted to mean that a person who has the right to purchase outstanding shares from a shareholder, such as on the death of the shareholder, will be deemed to own the number of shares he or she has the option to acquire. This could present a trap for the unwary, since there is no abuse presented by an option to acquire already-outstanding shares (because this will not dilute the ESOP).

The regulations interpreting Section 409(p) provide helpful guidance by providing that a right to acquire stock of an S corporation that is held by persons other than the ESOP, the S corporation, or a related entity does not constitute synthetic equity.[84] Therefore, a disqualified person should not be treated as owning shares that he or she may be entitled to purchase pursuant to the terms of a conventional buy-sell agreement or pursuant to any other similar agreement restricting the transferability of stock. However, the regulations also provide that although rights to acquire already-outstanding shares will not be treated as synthetic equity, a disqualified person may be treated as owning other

---

82. Treas. Reg. § 1.409(p)-1(c)(1).

83. Code § 409(p)(6)(C).

84. Treas. Reg. § 1.409(p)-1 (f)(2)(i).

shares that he or she has the right to purchase.[85] This provision of the regulations presumably covers options and other rights with respect to treasury shares or rights to be issued by the corporation in the future. Fortunately, the regulations go on to provide that a disqualified person will not be treated as owning shares that he or she may be entitled to purchase pursuant to the terms of a conventional buy-sell agreement, or pursuant to any other similar agreement restricting the transferability of stock, unless either (1) a principal purpose of the agreement is to circumvent the one-class-of-stock requirement for S corporations, or (2) the agreement establishes a purchase price that, at the time that the agreement is entered into, is significantly in excess of or below the fair market value of the stock.[86]

Stock Options

In the case of stock options and other forms of synthetic equity the value of which is determined by reference to and payable in shares of stock, the person who is entitled to the synthetic equity is treated as owning the number of shares of stock to be delivered pursuant to the terms of the synthetic equity agreement.[87] In the case of synthetic equity for which payment is made in cash or other property (besides stock of the S corporation), the number of shares of synthetic equity treated as owned by the holder of the synthetic equity is equal to that number of shares of stock having a value equal to the cash or other property to be delivered.[88] In the case of stock appreciation rights, the number of synthetic equity shares is equal to the appreciation in the value of the stock by reference to which the rights are valued.[89]

> ***Example 5.*** George is granted stock appreciation rights with respect to 1,000 shares of S corporation stock. At the time of the grant of the rights, the value of the stock is $10 per share. At a specified future date, George will be entitled to a benefit equal to the difference between the value of 1,000 shares of stock

85.   Treas. Reg. § 1.409(p)-1(c)(4)(i).

86.   Treas. Reg. § 1.409(p)-1(c)(4)(ii).

87.   Treas. Reg. § 1.409(p)-1(f)(4)(iii).

88.   Ibid.

89.   Ibid.

at that time and their value at the date of the grant of the rights. If the value of the stock is $12.50 per share on the determination date, George would be treated as holding 200 shares of synthetic equity (the value of the stock appreciation rights of $2.50 per share, or $2,500 in total, divided by the value of $12.50 per share on the determination date).

Special Rule Relating to Voting Rights

The regulations add a special rule relating to voting rights. If a synthetic equity right includes a right to purchase or receive shares of S corporation stock that have greater voting rights on a per-share basis than the shares held by the ESOP, then the number of deemed-owned shares attributable to the synthetic equity will be at least equal to the number of shares that would have the same voting rights if those shares had the same per-share voting rights as the voting rights of the shares held by the ESOP.[90]

> *Example 6.* If shares of S corporation stock held by an ESOP are entitled to one vote per share, then an individual who holds an option to purchase one share with 100 votes is treated as owning 100 shares of synthetic equity.

Proportionality Rule

The regulations also provide that the number of shares deemed to be owned by a holder of synthetic equity is to be determined on a proportionate basis where the ESOP does not own all of the stock of the S corporation.[91] The application of this rule can be illustrated by the following example:

> *Example 7.* Assume that an S corporation has 10,000 shares outstanding and that Helen owns 2,500 shares and the ESOP owns the remaining 7,500 shares. Assume that Ira would be treated as owning 200 synthetic equity shares but for the special rule provided for situations where the ESOP does not own all of the stock of the S corporation. The number of synthetic equity shares treated as owned by Ira is decreased from 200 to 150, because the ESOP owns only 75% of the outstanding stock of the corporation.

---

90. Treas. Reg. § 1.409(p)-1(f)(4)(v).
91. Treas. Reg. § 1.409(p)-1(f)(4)(iv).

Deferred Compensation

While the language of Section 409(p) limits the term "synthetic equity" to rights to acquire stock of the plan sponsor and rights to future cash payments based on the value of the stock of the plan sponsor, the regulations go further and provide that a deferred compensation arrangement will be treated as synthetic equity, even if it is neither payable in stock of the plan sponsor nor calculated by reference to the value of the stock of the plan sponsor.[92] The value of a deferred compensation arrangement is determined by converting the dollar value of the deferred compensation into an equivalent number of shares of stock in the plan sponsor, based on the present value of the interest or right to the deferred compensation and the fair market value of the plan sponsor's shares on the determination date.[93] Thus, if a participant has a deferred compensation program with a present value of $3 million and the current fair market value of a share of stock is $300, the number of shares of synthetic equity will be 10,000. If the value of a share of stock declines to $150 per share, the number of shares of synthetic equity will increase to 20,000. As you can see, a stark decrease in the stock value can adversely affect the Section 409(p) testing results. A special rule limits the need for continual revaluation of deferred compensation synthetic equity by permitting triennial determination dates.[94]

This expansion of the synthetic equity concept is a response by the Treasury Department to abuses of the S corporation ESOP rules that have been promoted by aggressive tax and insurance advisors. One common technique that has been promoted involves the use of management companies. In a typical scheme, the owners of a profitable company ("C") create a new management company ("M"), and the owner-employees of C become employees of M. M then enters into an agreement to provide management services to C, in consideration for a fee based on C's performance. M makes the S election for federal income tax purposes and adopts an ESOP, to which all of the stock of M is contributed or sold for a nominal amount. The ESOP covers all of the employees of both M and C. M then adopts a generous deferred

---

92. Treas. Reg. § 1.409(p)-1(f)(2)(iv).
93. Treas. Reg. § 1.409(p)-1(f)(4)(iii).
94. Treas. Reg. § 1.409(p)-1(f)(4)(ii)(C).

compensation program for its employees, who are the principal share-holders of C. Under this scheme, C will deduct the management fees that it pays to M, as business expenses, and M then will use the fees to fund its deferred compensation program.

The management fees received by M constitute taxable income; but because M is an S corporation wholly owned by an ESOP, neither M nor its sole shareholder (the ESOP) is liable for any taxes. In essence, the scheme is designed to enable the C/M combined entity to obtain a current deduction for funding the owners' deferred compensation program, something that ordinarily is not allowed under U.S. federal income tax laws. The resulting tax savings theoretically could be enormous. While the employees will participate in the ESOP, their benefits will be minimal because most of the profits from business operations will be diverted into the deferred compensation fund for the owners. The regulations eliminate this obvious abuse of the S corporation ESOP rules because the deferred compensation will be treated as synthetic equity. As a result, the executives covered by the deferred compensation program will be treated as disqualified persons, and each taxable year of the S corporation will be a nonallocation year.[95]

Prohibited Allocations

If there is a nonallocation year and Section 409(p) applies, then no shares of the company's stock may be allocated for that year to the accounts of any disqualified persons (and no other assets may be allocated to their accounts in lieu of company stock, either under the ESOP or under any other tax-qualified plan that the company sponsors).[96] The regulations provide that the Section 409(p) prohibition has two elements: (1) a prohibition on "accruals," and (2) a prohibition on "allocations." In explaining how these two prohibitions work, the regulations create two new terms: "impermissible accrual" and "impermissible allocation."[97] If there

---

95. For a more thorough discussion of this tax-avoidance technique and how it can be attacked by the IRS, see David Ackerman, "New Anti-Abuse Rules for S Corporation ESOPs," *ESOP Report*, July 2001.

96. Code § 409(p)(1).

97. Treas. Reg. § 1.409(p)-1(b)(2).

is either an impermissible accrual or an impermissible allocation, then there is a prohibited allocation within the meaning of Section 409(p).[98]

An impermissible accrual occurs if any S corporation stock owned by the ESOP, or any assets attributable to that stock, are held for the benefit of a disqualified person during a nonallocation year.[99] For example, any S corporation stock held in a disqualified person's account would be counted as an impermissible accrual, even if the stock already had been allocated in a prior year.[100] In addition, any distributions made on, and any proceeds from the sale of, S corporation stock would constitute impermissible accruals.[101] An impermissible allocation is any allocation for a disqualified person under any tax-qualified plan of the employer that occurs during a nonallocation year to the extent that an allocation is made that, but for a provision in the ESOP to comply with Section 409(p), would have been added to the account of the disqualified person under the ESOP and invested in S corporation securities owned by the ESOP.[102]

Penalties for Violation of the Nonallocation Rules

If prohibited allocations are made to disqualified persons, then the company will be subject to an excise tax equal to 50% of the amount of the prohibited allocations,[103] and the shares allocated to the accounts of the disqualified persons will be treated as having been distributed to the disqualified persons and they will be subject to tax on the value of those shares.[104] The regulations seem to imply that these penalties are imposed for each nonallocation year, regardless of whether anything is added to the disqualified person's account for that year,[105] although this result seems contrary to the general structure of the statute, which dif-

---

98.   Treas. Reg. § 1.409(p)-1(b)(2)(i).

99.   Treas. Reg. § 1.409(p)-1(b)(2)(ii).

100. Ibid.

101. Ibid.

102. Treas. Reg. § 1.409(p)-1(b)(2)(iii).

103. Code § 4979A(a).

104. Code § 409(p)(2)(A).

105. Treas. Reg. § 1.409(p)-1(b)(2)(i)-(iii).

ferentiates between the penalties for the initial nonallocation year and the penalties for subsequent nonallocation years.[106] The statute does not specify how shares that are deemed to have been distributed are to be treated in future years. If they are treated as continuing to be held by the persons to whom they were deemed to have been distributed, then those persons will be personally liable for tax on their proportionate share of the S corporation's income.

In addition to the penalties described above, it is possible that if prohibited allocations are made by an S corporation ESOP, the ESOP then may be disqualified. The law requires that the plan document must prohibit allocations to disqualified persons during nonallocation years, so any prohibited allocation would violate the plan document.[107] The IRS takes the position that violation of a plan document results in disqualification of the plan.[108] If an S corporation ESOP is disqualified, then the ESOP no longer would be a permitted holder of S corporation stock,[109] and the corporation's S election would be automatically terminated. There is a footnote in the legislative history of Section 409(p) which states that this result is not the congressional intent,[110] but it is not known what position the IRS would take on this matter.

Additional penalties will be imposed if any synthetic equity is owned by a disqualified person in any nonallocation year. Then the company will be subject to an excise tax equal to 50% of the value of the shares on which the synthetic equity is based.[111] It is important to note that the tax is imposed on the value of the shares to which the synthetic equity relates, and not the value of the synthetic equity itself.[112] Therefore, a substantial tax may be assessed even where the synthetic equity

---

106. See Code § 4979A(e)(2)(C), which imposes an excise tax during the first nonallocation year of an S corporation ESOP by taking into account the total value of all of the deemed-owned shares of all disqualified persons.

107. Code § 409(p)(1).

108. See, e.g., Rev. Proc. 2001-17, § 5.01(2), defining the term "Qualification Failure" as "any failure that adversely affects the qualification of a plan," including a failure to follow plan provisions.

109. Code § 1361(c)(6)(A).

110. House Conference Report 107-84, May 26, 2001, § VI.4(g), n. 122.

111. Code § 4974A(a)(4).

112. Code § 4979A(e)(2)(B).

itself is of little or no value, as for example where the strike price with respect to an option is equal to or greater than the fair market value of the stock covered by the option. The tax on synthetic equity appears to be especially onerous because the tax appears to be imposed on the same synthetic equity for every nonallocation year. For the first nonallocation year of an S corporation ESOP, a 50% excise tax will be applied against the total value of all of the deemed-owned shares of all of the disqualified persons, regardless of the amount actually allocated to their accounts during that year.[113]

Avoidance or Evasion of Section 409(p)

Section 409(p) of the Code authorizes the Treasury Department to issue regulations providing that a nonallocation year occurs in any case in which "the principal purpose of the ownership structure of an S corporation constitutes an avoidance or evasion of Section 409(p)."[114] Pursuant to this authority, the Treasury Department has set forth in the regulations the following standard for determining whether the principal purpose of the ownership structure of an S corporation involving synthetic equity constitutes an avoidance or evasion of Section 409(p): "whether, to the extent of the ESOP's stock ownership, the ESOP receives the economic benefits of ownership in the S corporation that occur during the period that stock of the S corporation is owned by the ESOP."[115] Among the factors identified in the regulations to be considered in determining whether the ESOP receives these economic benefits are shareholder voting rights, the right to receive distributions made to shareholders, and the right to benefit from the profits earned by the S corporation. In evaluating these factors, the regulations provide that there shall be taken into account the extent to which actual distributions of profits are made from the S corporation to the ESOP and the extent to which the ESOP's ownership interest in undistributed profits and future profits is subject to dilution as a result of synthetic equity.[116]

---

113. Code § 4979A(e)(2)(C).

114. Code § 409(p)(7)(B).

115. Treas. Reg. § 1.409(p)-(1)(g)(2).

116. Ibid.

The regulations go on to identify certain specific transactions that will be deemed to constitute an avoidance or evasion of Section 409(p). These transactions are the ones described in Revenue Ruling 2004-4, which involve fact patterns relating to the use of S corporation subsidiaries and other pass-through entities to enable certain individuals to benefit from the plan sponsor's S corporation status while limiting the ESOP's ability to benefit from the sponsor's profits.[117]

Prevention of Prohibited Allocations

There are several steps that might be taken by an S corporation that sponsors an ESOP to prevent an individual from becoming a disqualified person and to thereby avoid a nonallocation year. These measures include the following:

- reducing the amount of synthetic equity (for example, by canceling or distributing some or all of it);
- selling the S corporation stock held in the participant's ESOP account, so that the account is not invested in S corporation stock;
- distributing the S corporation stock held in the participant's account from the ESOP to the participant;
- transferring the S corporation stock held for the participant under the ESOP into a separate portion of the plan that is not an ESOP or to another qualified plan sponsored by the employer; or
- reshuffling account balances in a way designed to prevent participants from becoming disqualified persons.

A sale or distribution of S corporation stock allocated to a participant's account, or a transfer of S corporation stock allocated to a participant's account to another plan, might be deemed to violate the general nondiscrimination requirements applicable to all tax-qualified employee benefit plans. This is because the sale, distribution, or transfer would not be made generally available to all participants in the plan. The regulations provide relief from the nondiscrimination requirements for a transfer of S corporation stock from an ESOP to another

---

117. Treas. Reg. § 1.409(p)-(1)(h).

tax-qualified plan made for the purpose of assuring compliance with Section 409(p).[118] However, it should be noted that the other plan would be subject to unrelated business income tax on its share of the plan sponsor's income. ESOPs are the only type of employee benefit plans that are exempt from this tax.

Another possible approach would be to incorporate "fail-safe" language into an ESOP. This approach would require a change in the ESOP trust asset mix among participant accounts so as to not only prohibit allocations to disqualified persons during nonallocation years, but also to assure that the disqualified persons will not hold more than 50% of the total outstanding and deemed-owned shares of the corporation. This would work only with a careful review both of allocations of company stock within the ESOP and of ownership of company stock and of synthetic equity outside the ESOP. Just as a transfer of S corporation stock allocated from one participant's account to another plan might be deemed to violate the general nondiscrimination requirements applicable to all tax-qualified employee benefit plans, if only one or a few persons' accounts are affected by the reshuffling of account balances, the nondiscrimination requirements may be violated. The fact that the regulations specifically authorize a plan-to-plan transfer, but not a reshuffling of the plan assets, may give rise to an inference that the reshuffling technique is not exempt from the nondiscrimination requirements. It is important to note that as of this writing (fall 2014), the IRS's position is that transferring the S corporation stock held for the participant under the ESOP into a separate portion of the plan that is not an ESOP or to another qualified plan sponsored by the employer is the only acceptable method for avoiding a nonallocation year.

The S Corporation Election

Taxation of S Corporations and Their Shareholders

The primary effect of the S election is that all items of an S corporation's income and loss are passed through to the corporation's shareholders.[119] There is allocated to each shareholder his or her proportionate

---

118. Treas. Reg. § 1.409(p)-1(b)(2)(v)(B).

119. Code § 1366.

share of each item of corporate income, deduction, loss, and credit.[120] The S corporation itself generally will not be subject to federal income tax.[121] A shareholder's basis in his or her stock of an S corporation is increased by his or her share of the corporate income and is decreased by distributions received by the shareholder from the corporation and by his or her share of the corporation's items of loss and deduction.[122] A shareholder's basis in stock of an S corporation may not be reduced below zero.[123] Distributions from S corporations to their shareholders generally are tax-free to the extent of the shareholders' bases in their stock.[124] A shareholder will be subject to tax on any distribution to the extent that it exceeds his or her stock basis.[125]

Eligibility to Make S Election

Speaking generally, the following requirements must be met by a corporation for it to be eligible to make the S election:[126]

- The corporation may not have more than 100 shareholders.
- All shareholders must be U.S. citizens or U.S. residents, and they must be natural persons, estates, or certain types of trusts (including employee benefit trusts).
- The corporation may have only one class of stock outstanding (but different voting rights are permitted for different shares of stock).[127]

In addition, the following types of corporations are ineligible to make the S election: financial institutions that use the reserve method of accounting for bad debts; insurance companies; certain so-called "possession corporations" (corporations that derive most of their income

---

120. Code § 1366(a).
121. Code § 1363(a).
122. Code § 1367(a).
123. Code § 1367(a)(2).
124. Code § 1368(c).
125. Code § 1368(b)(2).
126. Code § 1361(b).
127. Code § 1361(c)(4).

from sources within a possession of the United States); and domestic international sales corporations (DISCs).[128]

Advantages of S Corporation Election

Avoidance of Double Tax

An important tax advantage of the S election is that only one tax is imposed on the earnings of an S corporation. C corporations are subject to a "double tax"—once at the corporate level[129] and again at the shareholder level when the after-tax corporate earnings are distributed to the shareholders.[130] Many closely held C corporations have been able to avoid the double tax by distributing earnings to their shareholders in the form of tax-deductible compensation.[131] However, this is not a complete answer to the double-tax problem for C corporations whose earnings exceed the amount that can be deemed to be "reasonable" compensation or for C corporations that have shareholders who are not actively involved in the conduct of their business operations. No deductions will be allowed to a corporation for salaries or bonuses paid to shareholder-employees that are in excess of a reasonable amount, with the result that the excessive "compensation" will be treated as a nondeductible dividend for federal income tax purposes.[132]

Tax Savings on the Sale or Liquidation of a Business

Shareholders of a C corporation are subject to a double tax upon a sale of their corporation's assets or a liquidation of their corporation. First, the corporation is subject to tax on the difference between the sale or liquidation proceeds and its basis in its assets,[133] and then the sharehold-

---

128. Code § 1361(b)(2).

129. Code § 11.

130. Code § 301.

131. See James P. Holden and A.L. Suwalsky, Jr., 202-3d T.M. *Reasonable Compensation,* and David Ackerman and Thomas J. Kinasz, "Tax Considerations in Organizing Closely Held Corporations," chapter 2 of *Closely Held Corporations* (Illinois Institute for Continuing Legal Education, 1990), at 2–12.

132. Ibid.

133. Code § 1001.

ers are subject to an additional tax on the distribution of the after-tax proceeds.[134] The effect may be illustrated by the following example:

> **Example 8.** Assume that a liquidating corporation sells its assets in 2014 at a gain of $1 million and that the shareholders' aggregate bases for their stock equals the corporation's basis for its assets. A 35% corporate tax will be imposed upon the gain, leaving the corporation with after-tax profits of $650,000. Upon the distribution of the proceeds to the shareholders, an additional tax in the amount of $154,700 will be imposed (23.8% of $650,000), leaving the shareholders with after-tax proceeds of $495,300.

If the corporation in the above example were an S corporation, only one tax would be imposed. The tax would be imposed upon the shareholders at a maximum rate of 23.8%, with the result that the total tax would be $238,000, as compared to $504,700, and the after-tax profit available to the shareholders would be $762,000, as compared to $495,300. Table 2-1 summarizes the comparison in tax results.

Table 2-1. Tax on sale of appreciated property and liquidation ($1,000,000 taxable gain)	
C corporation	
Corporate gain	$1,000,000
Corporate tax	(350,000)
After-tax corporate profit	650,000
Tax on distribution less basis (23.8% × $650,000)	(154,700)
After-tax profit	$ 495,300
Effective tax rate ([$1,000,000 − $495,300] ÷ $1,000,000)	50.47%
S corporation	
Corporate gain	$1,000,000
Corporate tax	(0)
After-tax corporate profit	1,000,000
Tax on distribution less basis (23.8% × $1,000,000)	(238,000)
After-tax profit	$ 762,000
Effective tax rate ([$1,000,000 − $762,000] ÷ $1,000,000)	23.8%

---

134. Code § 301.

If the transaction took the form of a liquidation, gain would be recognized by the corporation to the extent of the excess of the fair market value of its assets over the corporation's basis in its assets,[135] and the results would be the same. A double tax would be imposed on the C corporation and its shareholders, but only one level of tax would be imposed on the S corporation and its shareholders because the corporate gain would pass through to the shareholders, and their tax bases would be increased by the amount of the gain recognized.[136]

If the transaction took the form of a sale of stock, the corporate-level tax could be avoided even if the corporation had not made an S election, provided that the purchaser did not make an election under Section 338 of the Code to treat the transaction as a purchase of assets for federal income tax purposes. However, unless this election is made, the acquired corporation will not be entitled to step up the basis of its assets to the price paid for the stock. Then the amount of depreciation and amortization deductions to which the acquired corporation will be entitled in the future normally will be less than would be the case after a transaction structured as a purchase of assets.

On the other hand, if the purchaser makes the Section 338 election, the acquired corporation will be treated for tax purposes as if it had sold its assets and, as the new shareholder of the acquired corporation, the purchaser will bear the burden of the tax imposed on the constructive gain recognized by the acquired corporation. In order to both avoid this tax and obtain the benefit of a step-up in the basis of the acquired corporation's assets, a purchaser of a business normally will prefer to structure an acquisition as a purchase of assets and normally will pay a higher price for assets than for stock. Therefore, substantial benefits can be obtained by the owners of a corporation that will be sold by making an S election, even where it may be possible to arrange for a sale of their business in the form of a sale of stock.

To limit the benefits that can be obtained by converting a C corporation to an S corporation, Congress has enacted a corporate-level tax on S corporations that formerly were C corporations. This tax is imposed on any gain that arose before the effective date of the S elec-

---

135. Code § 336(a).

136. See footnotes 119–25 and accompanying text.

tion ("built-in" gain) and that is recognized by the S corporation within 10 years after the conversion by reason of a sale or distribution of its assets.[137] The built-in gain tax is assessed at a rate equal to the highest rate of corporate tax.[138] This tax applies in each year to the lesser of the S corporation's built-in gain or its taxable income.[139] Any recognized built-in gain not taxed by reason of the taxable-income limitation is carried forward to later tax years in which the S corporation has additional taxable income.[140]

To return to the above example, if the value of the assets of the corporation on the effective date of its S election had exceeded the corporation's basis in its assets by $500,000, it then would be subject to a corporate-level tax on $500,000 of the gain realized upon the sale of its assets. Because the built-in gain tax applies only to S corporations that previously were C corporations, the tax can be completely avoided if an S election is made at the time that a corporation is organized and is maintained in effect continually thereafter.

Pass-Through of Losses

Just as the earnings of an S corporation are "passed through" and taxed to its shareholders, so generally are its losses.[141] The shareholders may apply these losses to reduce their income from other sources, up to an amount equal to their tax bases in their stock.[142] Therefore, S elections often are made by owners of start-up ventures who desire the limited liability and other features of incorporation, and who anticipate that losses will be incurred at the outset of their operations.[143] Losses of

---

137. Code § 1374. Congress has considered, but not yet passed, legislation that would impose the tax at the time that the S election is made. Budget of the U.S. Govt., FY 1998, Legislative Proposals (1997).

138. Code § 1374(b)(1).

139. Code § 1374(d)(2).

140. Code § 1374(d)(2)(B).

141. Code § 1366.

142. Code § 1366(d).

143. For a potentially abusive use of S corporation ESOPs to take advantage of the pass-through of losses of a start-up venture, see Ginsburg, "The Taxpayer Relief Act of 1997: Worse Than You Think," *Tax Notes* 76 (Sept. 29, 1997): 1790.

a C corporation may be used only to offset prior or future corporate income.[144]

Valuation of S Corporation ESOP Stock

As mentioned above, ESOP-owned S corporations have a great tax advantage in that they can shelter all or part of their profits from taxes. A question arises as to whether that ability to shelter should be reflected in calculations of future earnings when determining the fair market value of the stock held by the ESOP. There is a consensus that appraisals should not reflect tax-effect earnings.[145] Arguably, the additional cash flow will increase earnings over time, but that can only be incorporated as the earnings occur, not as they would be projected to occur in the future. The reasoning is that no other buyer, except another ESOP-owned S corporation, could take advantage of these tax benefits, so the appraiser's calculation of projected earnings needs to reflect the taxes that the other buyer would pay but the ESOP sponsor does not.

The valuation issue also raises an interesting question regarding fiduciary duty. For example, if an ESOP trustee receives a proposal to purchase the company at a premium, should the trustee automatically agree to the purchase? Generally, there is support for the position that ESOP fiduciaries must consider the long-term benefits to the ESOP participants, not just gains that would be realized in one year, when considering a sale of the company.[146] The advantageous S corporation ESOP tax benefits mean that the fiduciary may conclude that the stock price increase may be so great that a current premium buyout of even 30% or more is insufficient.[147]

---

144. Code § 172(b).

145. Kathryn F. Aschwald and Donna J. Walker, "Valuing S Corporation ESOP Companies," chapter 4 in this book.

146. David Ackerman, *Questions and Answers on the Duties of ESOP Fiduciaries* (Oakland, CA: NCEO, 2008), 130–32.

147. Neil Brozen, "Responding to Unsolicited Offers to Purchase ESOP Companies: Issues for Plan Fiduciaries," in *Responding to ESOP Acquisition Offers* (Oakland, CA: NCEO, 2010), 15–20.

Acquisitions by S Corporation ESOPs

When a 100% ESOP-owned S corporation has paid off the ESOP loan, it often accumulates even more substantial cash, which can be used to grow the business, often in the form of acquiring other companies. Until the last several years, it was rare for ESOP companies to buy other companies. However, it has become quite common in recent years. At recent NCEO meetings, ESOP company representatives affirmatively responded when asked if they have recently acquired other companies or if they plan to acquire other companies in the near future.[148]

Other Benefits

Other benefits of the S election include the following: avoidance of the corporate alternative minimum tax;[149] reduction of the risks of a challenge by the IRS to the amount of compensation paid to shareholders;[150]

---

148. Corey Rosen and David Ackerman, "Recent Developments Making S Corporation ESOPs More Appealing," *Journal of Passthrough Entities* 15, vol. 5 (July/August 2012), 51–62.

149. Code § 1363(a). However, an S corporation shareholder may be subject to the alternative minimum tax as a result of the pass-through of items of tax preference of the S corporation. See Code § 1366(b).

150. Because an S corporation generally is not subject to the corporate tax, it generally makes no difference for tax purposes whether distributions to shareholders of S corporations are characterized as compensation or dividends. This does not mean, however, that there is no limit on the amount of compensation that may be paid to the corporation's officers. To the extent that the officers' compensation exceeds a reasonable amount, the shareholders of the corporation may be able to impose limits under applicable corporate laws. The board of directors of a corporation must act in the best interests of the shareholders in managing the affairs of the corporation, and directors who approve excessive officer compensation may be held liable for mismanagement. Where some or all of the shares of a corporation are held by an ESOP, the ESOP trustee should monitor the actions of the board of directors. Among other things, the ESOP trustee should evaluate the amount of compensation being paid to the officers. To the extent that the officers' compensation is excessive, corporate earnings to which the ESOP and the other shareholders otherwise would be entitled are being drained off to the officers. In that case, the ESOP trustee would have an obligation to take action to protect the interests of the ESOP. If necessary, the ESOP trustee might have a duty to bring a shareholders' derivative action against the directors. For a thorough discussion of the du-

avoidance of the accumulated earnings tax;[151] and the availability of the cash method of accounting.[152]

Disadvantages of S Corporation Election

Shareholder Limitations

An S corporation may have no more than 100 shareholders.[153] This may require a corporation to closely monitor and control the distribution of its stock. In addition, some investors may be frustrated by the limitations on the kinds of trusts that may hold stock of an S corporation.

One-Class-of-Stock Limitation

The one-class-of-stock limitation restricts planning options for the capital structure of an S corporation. For example, no preferred stock can be issued by an S corporation to outside investors. However, the issuance by an S corporation of most types of stock options, stock warrants, or convertible debentures generally will not constitute the creation of a second class of stock.[154] Many existing ESOP companies have capital structures that include convertible preferred stock or so-called "super" common stock, in addition to regular common stock. These kinds of shares often are issued where it is anticipated that dividends

---

ties of an ESOP trustee in connection with the monitoring of management compensation, see David Ackerman, "Questions and Answers Regarding the Legal Responsibilities of ESOP Fiduciaries," *Journal of Employee Ownership Law & Finance* 13, no. 1 (winter 2001): 1, 31–32.

151. Code § 1363(a). Because S corporations generally are not subject to federal income tax and business earnings of an S corporation are taxed to the shareholders whether or not distributed, there is no reason to penalize accumulations of income in an S corporation.

152. Most regular corporations with annual gross receipts in excess of $5 million are prohibited from using the cash method of accounting. Code § 448. However, limitations on the use of the cash method of accounting do not apply to S corporations. Code § 448(a).

153. Code § 1361(b)(1)(A).

154. Rev. Rul. 67-269, 1967-2 Cum. Bull. 298. See, e.g., Treas. Regs. §§ 1361-1(b)(4), 1361-1(l)(4)(iii). See discussion above at footnotes 56–63. See also David Ackerman, "Stock Options for S Corporations," *Journal of Employee Ownership Law and Finance* 13, no. 3 (summer 2001): 55.

will be used to pay off an ESOP loan because the annual loan payments exceed the maximum amount that may be contributed to the plan on a tax-deductible basis. In this situation, it generally is desirable to limit the dividends to shares held by the ESOP. In this way, the dividend cost can be limited, and double taxation on dividends that otherwise would be payable to other shareholders can be avoided.[155] Where a C corporation has created a second class of stock for these reasons, it may not be feasible to make the S election, which would require the elimination of the special class of stock created for the ESOP.

Limitation on Other Benefits

Persons who own 2% or more of the outstanding shares of an S corporation may not exclude from their income the value of fringe benefits that are provided to them.[156] Examples of these types of benefits include group term life insurance, certain health and accident plans, death benefits, and meals and lodging reimbursement.

Fiscal Year

The taxable year of an S corporation must be the calendar year, unless the corporation can establish, to the satisfaction of the IRS, a business purpose for using a different fiscal year.[157] Not surprisingly, the deferral of income to stockholders for a limited period of time will not be

---

155. For discussions of the use of "super" common and convertible preferred stocks in ESOPs, see Gregory K. Brown and Kim Schultz Abello, "ESOPs and Security Design: Common Stock, Super Common, or Convertible Preferred?" *Journal of Pension Planning & Compliance* 23 (1997): 99, and Jared Kaplan, "Is ESOP a Fable? Fabulous Uses and Benefits or Phenomenal Pitfalls?" *Taxes* 65 (1987): 792–93.

156. Code § 1372.

157. Code §§ 444, 1378. An example of a business purpose that will be accepted for adopting a taxable year other than the calendar year is a change to a tax year that coincides with the corporation's "natural business year." A taxable year will be deemed to be a natural business year if 25% or more of the corporation's gross receipts in each of the last three 12-month periods proposed to serve as the taxable year have been recognized in the last two months of those periods. Rev. Proc. 83-25 § 4.04, 1983-1 C.B. 689, 692.

treated as a business purpose.[158] However, an S corporation may adopt a taxable year other than the calendar year if shareholders holding more than one-half of the shares of the corporation have the same tax year or are changing to the corporation's tax year.[159] This means that if an ESOP holds more than one-half of the outstanding shares of an S corporation, the S corporation may adopt the same taxable year as the ESOP, even if that year is not the calendar year. Where the principal shareholders of an S corporation are changing to a new tax year to be adopted by the corporation, the shareholders may not change their tax year without first obtaining approval from the IRS.[160] There is an exception to the general rule under which an S corporation may elect to adopt a tax year ending not earlier than September 30.[161] In that case, however, payments in the nature of advance tax deposits are required, which takes away the advantage of the tax deferral.[162]

State Tax Considerations

Although most states recognize S corporation status for purposes of their tax laws, not all states follow the federal pattern. Some states tax S corporations and not their shareholders; some states tax both the S corporation and its shareholders; and some states do not tax either the corporation or the shareholders. If the S election is made by a corporation that is incorporated in a state that does not follow the federal rules regarding the tax treatment of S corporations or that has modified them, difficult state tax compliance programs can arise, especially if multi-state operations are involved.[163]

---

158. Code § 1378(b).

159. Rev. Proc. 83-25 § 4.02, 1983-1 C.B. 689.

160. Ibid.

161. Code § 444(b).

162. Code §§ 444(c)(1), 7519.

163. For a thorough discussion of this issue, see Maule, *S Corporations: State Law and Taxation* (Deerfield, IL: Callaghan, 1992). Also see chapter 3 of this book, "A State-by-State Analysis of S Corporation Tax Treatment."

Conclusion

Enormous tax savings are possible for corporations that make the S election for federal income tax purposes and adopt an ESOP. These tax benefits are maximized where all of the outstanding shares of the corporation are held by the ESOP. The NCEO estimates that about half of the roughly 7,000 ESOPs that exist are sponsored by S corporations and that the large majority of these either are or will become 100% ESOP-owned. This trend can be expected to continue as understanding of the tax incentives created for ESOP-owned S corporations increases. As the number of ESOP-owned S corporations expands, however, Congress may reexamine the tax incentives that it has provided for this form of business ownership. However, to date, the anti-abuse rules of Section 409(p) have worked well. S corporations with few employees are unable to use ESOPs, and Section 409(p) prevents the creation of capital structures in ESOP-owned S corporations that can result in excessive dilution to the ESOP. As a result, the congressional policy of promoting broad-based employee ownership is being fulfilled by the increase in the number of ESOP-owned S corporations.

Chapter 3

A State-by-State Analysis of S Corporation Tax Treatment

Brian Hector[1]

An S corporation generally is not subject to federal income tax.[2] Instead, the shareholders of the corporation are subject to tax on the corporation's earnings, whether they are distributed to them as dividends or retained in the corporation.[3] Each shareholder is allocated his or her proportionate share of each item of corporate income, deduction, loss, and credit.[4] An important tax advantage of the S election is that only one tax is imposed on the earnings of an S corporation. Regular or C corporations present the challenge of a "double tax"—earnings are taxed once at the corporate level and again at the shareholder level when the after-tax corporate earnings are distributed to shareholders.

Historically, ESOPs were not eligible to hold shares of an S corporation. In 1996 the definition of an S corporation's eligible shareholders was expanded to include certain tax-exempt entities.[5] This change allowed for shareholders of ESOP companies to make the S election. Where a

---

1. The author would like to acknowledge the help and assistance of Daniel Carmody, Matthew Gregoline, and Jon Robin, who all provided significant contributions to this chapter. The original version of this chapter in the previous edition of this book was written by Renee Lewis.
2. Internal Revenue Code ("Code") § 1363(a).
3. Code § 1366.
4. Code § 1366(a).
5. Code § 1361(c)(6).

shareholder is an ESOP that is a tax-exempt trust,[6] any earnings attributable to the ESOP as a shareholder in the S corporation are tax-free.[7]

Although most states recognize the federal S corporation election for purposes of their income tax laws, many states impose additional requirements for state purposes. For example, some states require a notice to be filed at the state level; some states allow corporations to opt out of federal S corporation treatment for state purposes; and some states require a separate state S corporation election to be made.

Once an S corporation election has been made, the tax treatment of the S corporation varies by state. Most states exempt an S corporation from income tax, but some states impose an income tax on the corporation (although often at a reduced rate). Even where a state exempts an S corporation from taxation, the state will frequently follow the federal provisions for taxes on built-in gains and passive investment income under Code Sections 1374 and 1375. Furthermore, most states do not exempt S corporations from franchise taxes based on net worth, and many states impose a franchise tax on S corporations that operate as financial institutions.

States often adopt specific procedures to enforce pass-through taxation against nonresident shareholders. In some cases, this may require a formal consent to the state's taxing jurisdiction from the nonresident shareholder. In other cases, the corporation's S status may be contingent on the nonresident shareholders filing the appropriate state returns. Alternatively, this may involve a withholding regime or "tax" at the corporate level that is based on the nonresident shareholder's proportionate share of income. These mechanisms are not always relevant for an S corporation that is wholly owned by an ESOP (due to the ESOP's tax-exempt status) and so are beyond the scope of this chapter. However, it is a best practice to review these potential state mechanisms, particularly when there are shareholders other than the ESOP.[8]

---

6. Code § 501(a).

7. Code § 512(e) generally requires tax exempt shareholders to treat their proportionate share of an S corporation's income as unrelated business taxable income, but ESOPs receive an exemption from this rule.

8. A state tax withholding mechanism may present concerns with regard to the "single class of stock" requirement of Code Section 1361(b)(1)(C). A state tax withholding regime will not generally create a second class of stock, but

Corporations may also need to consider the state tax treatment of qualified subchapter S subsidiaries ("QSubs").[9] A subsidiary is a QSub if the following requirements are met: (1) the subsidiary is a domestic corporation, (2) the subsidiary is not otherwise disqualified under Code Section 1361(b)(2), (3) 100% of the stock of the subsidiary is owned by an S corporation, and (4) the S corporation parent elects to treat the subsidiary as a QSub.[10] When an election to treat a subsidiary as a QSub is made, all assets, liabilities, and items of income, deduction, and credit of the QSub are treated as the assets, liabilities, and items of income of the parent S corporation.[11]

Corporations considering making an election to be treated as an S corporation should be aware of the state tax consequences before making the election. The question whether a shareholders of an ESOP company should make an S election must be analyzed on a case-by-case basis, taking into consideration not only the federal tax benefits but also the tax consequences under state law.

This chapter presents an overview of the tax treatment of S corporations in each state. Table 3-1 sets forth (1) whether a state recognizes the concept of an S corporation for income tax purposes, (2) whether a state requires a separate state-level S election, (3) whether a state follows the federal treatment of QSubs, (4) whether a state that acknowledges S corporations nevertheless has significant deviations from the federal treatment, and (5) whether there are any corporate-level taxes (apart from the income tax) that may apply for an S corporation.[12] The table is current as of July 1, 2014.

---

withholdings will be considered constructive distributions, and the corporation must allow for equalizing actual distributions to resident shareholders to comply with the single class of stock requirement. Treas. Reg. § 1.1361-1(l)(2)(ii).

9. Many states still use the prior federal acronym of "QSSSs" to refer to QSubs. This chapter uses "QSub" or "QSubs" uniformly to avoid confusion.

10. Code § 1361(b)(3)(B).

11. Code § 1361(b)(3)(A)(iii).

12. In addition to the taxes identified, some states may characterize their non-resident withholding mechanisms as a corporate-level "tax."

Table 3-1. State-by-state analysis

State	S corporations recognized for state income tax purposes	Separate state-level S election	State follows federal treatment of qualified subchapter S subsidiaries (QSubs)	State-specific considerations	Imposition of other state taxes on S corporations
Alabama[1]	Yes	No	Yes		Subject to AL business privilege tax.
Alaska[2]	Yes	No	Yes	No apparent corporate level tax for built-in gains or excess passive investment income.	Subject to biennial corporation license tax.
Arizona[3]	Yes	No	Yes		
Arkansas[4]	Yes	Yes	Yes		Subject to AR franchise tax.
California[5]	Yes	No	Yes	Full pass through for shareholders; reduced tax rate at corporate level (1.5%–3.5%) for most income; full tax rate at corporate level for built-in gains and passive investment income.	Subject to CA franchise tax at a reduced rate (minimum franchise tax of $800).
Colorado[6]	Yes	No	Yes	No tax on built-in gains or passive investment income.	

Table 3-1. State-by-state analysis

State	S corporations recognized for state income tax purposes	Separate state-level S election	State follows federal treatment of qualified subchapter S subsidiaries (QSubs)	State-specific considerations	Imposition of other state taxes on S corporations
Connecticut[7]	Yes	No	Yes	No tax on built-in gains or passive investment income.	Subject to the $250 CT business entity tax (note: S corporation also responsible for CT business entity tax for any QSubs).
Delaware[8]	Yes	No	Yes	No tax on built-in gains or passive investment income.	Subject to business license and excise taxes.
District of Columbia[9]	No (an S corporation under federal law is treated as a regular corporation for DC purposes).	N/A	N/A	N/A	Corporations also subject to the annual ballpark fee.
Florida[10]	Yes	No	Yes		Subject to annual fee and annual supplemental corporate fee.

Table 3-1. State-by-state analysis

State	S corporations recognized for state income tax purposes	Separate state-level S election	State follows federal treatment of qualified subchapter S subsidiaries (QSubs)	State-specific considerations	Imposition of other state taxes on S corporations
Georgia[11]	Yes	Can depend on certain facts: generally no, but nonresident shareholders must execute a Form 600S-CA consent or else Georgia does not recognize election for any shareholder.	Yes (treatment applies for income tax purposes but not for net worth tax purposes).		S corporations are subject to net worth tax.
Hawaii[12]	Yes	No	Yes		S corporation that is a financial corporation under HI law is subject to HI bank franchise tax.
Idaho[13]	Yes	No	Yes		N/A
Illinois[14]	Yes	No	Yes		Subject to IL replacement tax at a reduced rate; subject to franchise tax.
Indiana[15]	Yes	No	Yes		

Table 3-1. State-by-state analysis

State	S corporations recognized for state income tax purposes	Separate state-level S election	State follows federal treatment of qualified subchapter S subsidiaries (QSubs)	State-specific considerations	Imposition of other state taxes on S corporations
Iowa[16]	Yes	No	Yes		S corporation that is a financial institution is subject to the IA financial institution franchise tax.
Kansas[17]	Yes	No	Yes		S corporations that are banks and savings and loan associations are subject to KS bank privilege tax rather than KS income tax.
Kentucky[18]	Yes	No	Yes		Subject to limited liability entity tax.
Louisiana[19]	No	N/A	Yes (if QSub qualifies for exclusion, S corporation that owns stock of QSub files a LA income tax return that includes all income of QSub).	An S corporation may exclude the percentage of its Louisiana net income on which its shareholders have paid Louisiana taxes.	Subject to franchise tax.
Maine[20]	Yes	No	Yes		S corporations that are financial institutions are subject to franchise tax.

Table 3-1. State-by-state analysis

State	S corporations recognized for state income tax purposes	Separate state-level S election	State follows federal treatment of qualified subchapter S subsidiaries (QSubs)	State-specific considerations	Imposition of other state taxes on S corporations
Maryland[21]	Yes	No	Yes		
Massachusetts[22]	Yes	No	Yes	S corporations subject to a corporate excise tax. There are separate tax law provisions applicable to S corporations depending on type of corporation. Generally, an entity with less than $6 million in gross receipts is not taxable on excise tax income base and an entity with $6 million or more in gross receipts is subject to corporate excise tax (measured by net income) at a reduced rate.	Generally, subject to the excise tax (not measured by net income) or, if applicable, the minimum excise tax.

Table 3-1. State-by-state analysis

State	S corporations recognized for state income tax purposes	Separate state-level S election	State follows federal treatment of qualified subchapter S subsidiaries (QSubs)	State-specific considerations	Imposition of other state taxes on S corporations
Michigan[23]	Yes	No	Yes	S corporation that is a financial institution or insurance company is subject to corporate income tax.	
Minnesota[24]	Yes	No	Yes		Subject to minimum fee.
Mississippi[25]	Yes	Yes (within 60 days of filing federal Form 2553).	Yes	No apparent tax on built-in gains or excess passive investment income.	Subject to franchise tax.
Missouri[26]	Yes	No	Yes		Subject to franchise tax.
Montana[27]	Yes	No	Yes	Grandfather provision allows certain federal "S" corporations to be taxed as regular corporations for state purposes.	

Table 3-1. State-by-state analysis

State	S corporations recognized for state income tax purposes	Separate state-level S election	State follows federal treatment of qualified subchapter S subsidiaries (QSubs)	State-specific considerations	Imposition of other state taxes on S corporations
Nebraska[28]	Yes	No	Yes	Built-in gains and excess passive income apparently not subject to tax.	S corporation that is a financial institution may be subject to financial institution tax if certain requirements met.
Nevada	Nevada does not impose an income tax on businesses.	N/A	N/A	N/A	N/A
New Hampshire[29]	No (S corporation under federal law treated same as regular corporation) for business profits tax purpose.	N/A	No (QSub under federal law treated as a regular S corporation for business profits tax purposes, and must file its own return unless part of a combined return).	Taxable based on recomputed taxable income under state law.	May also be subject to business enterprise tax based upon enterprise value.
New Jersey[30]	Yes	Yes. Taxed as C corporation in the absence of separate state election.	Yes (QSub must meet certain additional election requirements under NJ law).		S corporations as defined in IRC §1361 are subject to the franchise tax at special tax rate.
New Mexico[31]	Yes	No	Yes		Subject to franchise tax.

Table 3-1. State-by-state analysis

State	S corporations recognized for state income tax purposes	Separate state-level S election	State follows federal treatment of qualified subchapter S subsidiaries (QSubs)	State-specific considerations	Imposition of other state taxes on S corporations
New York[32]	Yes	Yes	Generally yes, but may require a separate inclusion election if QSub not a NY taxpayer.	New York does not have a special tax for built-in gains or excess passive income.	For tax years beginning before January 1, 2015, New York imposes a separate tax regime on banking corporations; S corporations are subject to fixed minimum tax.
Nevada	N/A (no corporate tax)	N/A	N/A	N/A	N/A
North Carolina[33]	Yes	No	Yes	Built-in gains and excess passive income not subject to tax.	Subject to franchise tax.
North Dakota[34]	Yes	No	Yes		
Ohio[35]	Yes	Yes – FT 1120-S, Notice of S Corporation Status must be filed annually.	Yes	Built-in gains and excess passive income not subject to tax.	Subject to commercial activity tax.

Table 3-1. State-by-state analysis

State	S corporations recognized for state income tax purposes	Separate state-level S election	State follows federal treatment of qualified subchapter S subsidiaries (QSubs)	State-specific considerations	Imposition of other state taxes on S corporations
Oklahoma[36]	Yes	No	Yes	Built-in gains and excess passive income not subject to tax.	Subject to franchise tax.
Oregon[37]	Yes	No	Yes		Subject to a $150 minimum tax.
Pennsylvania[38]	Yes	No (subject to ability to opt out of PA S corporation status).	Yes	Excess passive income not subject to tax.	Subject to capital stock and franchise tax (expires December 31, 2015).
Rhode Island[39]	Yes	No	Yes		Subject to franchise tax (repealed effective January 1, 2015); subject to minimum tax.
South Carolina[40]	Yes	No (with certain grandfather rules for corporations with a federal S election before 1985).	Yes	Built-in gains and excess passive income apparently not subject to tax.	Subject to the corporate license tax.

Table 3-1. State-by-state analysis

State	S corporations recognized for state income tax purposes	Separate state-level S election	State follows federal treatment of qualified subchapter S subsidiaries (QSubs)	State-specific considerations	Imposition of other state taxes on S corporations
South Dakota	SD does not impose a tax measured by net income on businesses or individuals. Net income tax is imposed on financial institutions (even if S corporations).	N/A	N/A	N/A	N/A
Tennessee[41]	No	N/A	No (QSub must file its own separate entity excise tax election).	Taxable (excise tax).	Subject to franchise tax.
Texas[42]	No	N/A	No	Subject to franchise margin tax.	
Utah[43]	Yes	No	Yes		
Vermont[44]	Yes	No	Yes		Subject to minimum tax of $250.
Virginia[45]	Yes	No	Yes		

Table 3-1. State-by-state analysis

State	S corporations recognized for state income tax purposes	Separate state-level S election	State follows federal treatment of qualified subchapter S subsidiaries (QSubs)	State-specific considerations	Imposition of other state taxes on S corporations
Washington[46]	WA does not impose an income tax on businesses or individuals.	N/A	N/A	N/A	Subject to business and occupation tax and corporate license fee.
West Virginia[47]	Yes	No	Yes	Built-in gains and excess passive income apparently not taxed.	Subject to franchise tax.
Wisconsin[48]	Yes	No (subject to ability to elect out of S status).	Yes	Excess passive income apparently not taxed.	Subject to WI economic development surcharge as a percentage of net income; corporate franchise tax on interest income from U.S. obligations.
Wyoming[49]	WY does not impose an income tax on businesses or individuals.	N/A	N/A	N/A	Subject to corporate license tax.

Notes to Table 3-1

1. Ala. Code § 40-18-160 (S corporation—definition and exemption); Ala. Code § 40-14A-22 (business privilege tax).

2. Alaska Stat. § 43.20.021 (Internal Revenue Code adopted by reference); Alaska Stat. § 10.06.845 (biennial corporation license tax).

3. Ariz. Rev. Stat. Ann. § 43-1126 (small business corporation); Ariz. Rev. Stat. Ann. §43-102 (conformity statute); 2013 Form 120S Instructions (addressing QSubs as disregarded entities).

4. Ark. Code Ann. § 26-51-409 (Subchapter S as in effect for January 1, 2013, adopted in Arkansas, separate state-level election); Ark. Code. Ann. § 26-54-104 (annual franchise tax).

5. Cal. Rev. & Tax. Cd. § 23802 (rates and exceptions for S corporations); Cal. Rev. & Tax. Cd. §23800.5 (providing for QSubs); Cal. Rev. & Tax. Cd. § 23809 (tax on built-in gains); Cal. Rev. & Tax. Cd. § 23811 (passive investment income); Cal. Rev. & Tax. Cd. § 23153 ($800 fixed dollar minimum tax).

6. Colo. Rev. Stat. § 39-22-103(10.5) (defining S corporation); Colo. Rev. Stat. § 39-22-302 (S corporation not subject to tax); Colo. Rev. Stat. § 39-22-322 (taxation of an S corporation and its shareholders).

7. Conn. Gen. Stat. § 12-213(a)(22) (defining S corporation as including QSub); Conn. Gen. Stat. §12-214(a)(2)(J) (S corporations exempted from corporate tax); Conn. Gen. Stat., § 12-284b (business entity tax).

8. Del. Code Ann. tit. 30 § 1621 (taxation of pass-through entities); Del. Code. Ann. tit. 30 §1902(b)(9) (exempting S corporation from corporate level income tax); Del. Income Tax Reg. 1.900.2(c) (providing for QSubs).

9. D.C. Code Ann. § 47-1801.04(10) (defines "corporation" as specifically including Federal S corporations); D.C. Code Ann. § 47-1807.02 (tax rates on corporations); D.C. Code Ann. §47-2762 (annual ballpark fee).

10. Fla. Stat. Ann. § 220.02(9) (addressing QSubs); Fla. Admin. Code Ann. § 12C-1.022(1)(b)(1) (S corporation not subject to tax); Fla. Admin. Code Ann. §12C-1.013(1)(d) (S corporation subjection to built-in gains tax and passive investment income tax); Fla. Stat. §607.0122 (annual fee); Fla. Stat. §607.193(1) (annual supplemental corporate fee).

11. Ga. Code Ann. § 4 48-7-21(b)(7)(B) (taxation of corporations—S election contingent on nonresident shareholders paying tax); Ga. Comp. R. & Regs. § 560-7-3-.06(6)(a) (net worth tax); 2013 Form IT-611S Instructions (signaling possible application of corporate level tax for built-in gains and excess passive income).

12. Haw. Rev. Stat. § 235-2.45(h) (adoption of Subchapter S); Haw. Rev. Stat. § 235-122(a)-(b) (federal S and QSub elections respected); Haw. Rev. Stat. § 241-3 (financial companies tax).

13. Idaho Code § 63-3004 (conformity statue); Idaho Code § 63-3030(a)(4) (federal S election followed); Idaho Admin. Rules 35.01.01.285 (QSub treatment).

14. ILCS Chapter 35 § 5/1501(a)(28) (S election); ILCS Chapter 35 § 5/2051(c) (S corporation exempt); ILCS Chapter 35 § 5/201(c) (personal property tax replacement income tax).

15. Ind. Code § 6-3-2-2.8(2) (follow federal S treatment): Indiana Revenue Ruling No. IT 02-01 (federal QSub status followed).

16. Iowa Code § 422.36(5) (follows federal S treatment); Iowa Code § 422.60 (franchise tax); Iowa Admin. Code § 701-52.1(5) (federal QSub status followed).

17. Kan. Stat. Ann. § 79-32,139 (federal S treatment followed); Kan. Stat. Ann. § 79-1106 (banking privilege tax).

18. Ky. Rev. Stat. Ann. § 141.206(11) (federal S election followed); Ky. Rev. Stat. Ann. §141.040(1)(i) (generally exempt); Ky. Rev. Stat. Ann § 141.0401(2) (limited liability entity tax); 2013 Form 720S Instructions (acknowledge federal QSub status followed).

19. La. Rev. Stat. Ann. § 47:287.732 (federal S concepts not followed except for limited "S corporation exclusion" and ability to treat federal QSub as disregarded for Louisiana purposes); La. Rev. Stat. Ann § 47:601 (franchise tax).

20. Me. Rev. Stat. Ann. tit. 36, § 111(1-A) (conformity provision); Me. Rev. Stat. Ann. tit. 36, § 5102(10) (taxation of federal S corporations); Me. Rev. Stat. Ann. tit. 36, § 5206 (franchise tax on financial institutions).

21. Md. Code Ann. Tax-Gen § 10-101(l) (follows federal S election), Md. Code Ann. Tax-Gen § 10-104(6) (S corporation generally exempt), §10-102.1, Md. Code Ann. Tax-Gen § 10-304(3) (incorporates built-in gains and excess passive income tax); 2013 Form 510 Instructions—Pass Through Entity Income Tax Return (follow federal QSub status).

22. Mass. Gen. L. § 39 (imposition of excise tax on business corporations); Mass. Gen. L. § 32D (S corporations; determination of net income measure of excise); Mass. Gen. Law Chapter 63 § 2 (imposition of excise tax on financial corporation; Mass. Gen. Law Chapter 63 § 38B (imposition of tax on a securities corporation).

23. Mich. Comp Laws Ann. § 206.623 (imposition of tax); Mich. Comp Laws Ann. §§206.605 & 206.611 (defining taxpayer and corporation); Mich. Comp Laws Ann. §206.699 (follow federal QSub status).

24. Minn. Stat. § 290.9725 (defines exemption for federal S corporation), Minn. Stat. § 290.9727 (tax imposed on certain IRC 1374 built-in gain), Minn. Stat. § 290.0922 (minimum fee); Minn. Stat. § 290.9729 (tax on passive investment income); Minnesota Revenue Notice No. 13-01 (federal QSub status followed).

25. Miss. Code Ann. § 27-8-3(1)(g) (defining S corporation); Miss. Code Ann. § 27-7-5(2) (imposition of tax); Miss. Code Ann. § 27-8-7(1) (S corporation exemption from income tax); Miss Code Ann. § 27-13-1(c) (definitions); Miss

Code Ann. § 27-13-5(1) (domestic corporation franchise tax); Miss Code Ann. § 27-13-7(1) (foreign corporation franchise tax); Miss. Administrative Code 35.III.8.03 (special rules for S corporations; conforms with federal QSub status).

26. Mo. Rev. Stat. § 143.431 (ties Missouri taxable income to federal); Mo. Rev. Stat. § 143.471(1) (S corporation exemption from income tax and other S corporation provisions including shareholder withholding); Mo. Rev. Stat. § 147.010(1) (imposition of franchise tax).

27. Mont. Code Ann. § 15-30-3301 (S corporation defined) & § 15-30-3302(1)(b) (S corporation exempt from tax); Mont. Code Ann. § 15-30-3313 (nonresident withholding or consent to tax); Mont. Admin. R. §42.9.520 (information reporting for QSubs).

28. Neb. Rev. Stat. §77-2734.02 (imposition of corporation income tax); Neb. Rev. Stat. §77-2734.04(9) (a corporate taxpayer does not include a corporation with a federal S election in effect); Neb. Rev. Stat. § 77-2734.01(1) (treatment of S corporation shareholders); Neb. Rev. Stat. § 77-3801(4) (defines financial institution for franchise tax on financial institutions); Neb. Rev. Stat. § 77-3802(1) (imposition of financial intuitions franchise tax); 2013 Form 1120-SN Instructions (federal QSub status followed).

29. N.H. Rev. Stat. Ann. § 77-A:1 (income tax definitions); N.H. Rev. Stat. Ann. § 77-E:2 (imposition of business enterprise tax); N.H. Rev. Stat. Ann. § 77-E:1 (business enterprise tax definitions); N.H. Admin. Rules, Rev. § 302.01(a)-(b) (reporting for corporations with federal QSub election in effect).

30. N.J. Rev. Stat. § 54:10A-5:22(a) (election as a New Jersey S corporation); N.J. Rev. Stat § 54:10A-5(c)(2) (imposition of franchise tax); N.J. Admin. Code § 18:7-20.2 (QSub treatment); N.J. Admin. Code § 18:7-1.18 (definition of S corporation).

31. NMSA § 7-2A-2(G) (conformity statute), NMSA § 7-2A-3(B) (imposition of franchise tax).

32. N.Y. Tax Law § 208(1-A) (definition of a general business corporation New York S corporation); N.Y. Tax Law § 210.1(g) (calculation of business tax for New York S corporation); N.Y. Tax Law § 210.1 (fixed minimum tax); N.Y. Tax Law § 208(1-B) (definition of New York QSub); N.Y. Tax Law § 660(a)-(b) (New York S corporation election); N.Y. Tax Law 1450(f) (definition of a banking corporation New York S corporation); N.Y. Tax Law 1450(g), (definition of a banking corporation New York QSub); N.Y. Tax Law 1455(c) (calculation of banking corporation New York S corporation tax).

33. N.C. Gen. Stat. § 105-114(b)(2) (defines corporation for imposition of franchise tax); N.C. Gen. Stat. § 105-122(a) (imposition of franchise tax); N.C. Gen. Stat. § 105-130.3 (S corporation exempt from tax on corporations); N.C. Gen. Stat. § 105-131.1(a) (S corporation exempt from tax on corporations); NC Gen. Stat. § 105-131(b)(8); N.C. Gen. Stat. § 105-228.90(1)(b) (Internal Revenue Code

conformity including QSub treatment); N.C. Gen. Stat. § 105-131.7 (returns; shareholder agreements; mandatory withholding).

34. N.D. Cent. Code § 57-38-01.1 (recognition of S election at federal level); N.D. Cent. Code § 57-38-01.4(1) (recognition of subchapter S election).

35. Ohio Rev. Code Ann. §5733.09(B) (corporation with federal S election is exempt from franchise tax; must file annual exemption notice); Ohio Rev. Code Ann § 51.01(A), § 5751.02 (commercial activity tax).

36. Okla. Stat. § 2365 (federal S election results in exemption from all state income tax); Okla. Admin. Code § 710: 40-1-15 (S corporations are subject to franchise tax).

37. Ore. Rev. Stat. § 314.730(2) (federal S election is followed); Ore. Rev. Stat. § 314.732(1) (S corporation generally exempt); Ore. Rev. Stat. § 314.740 (tax on built-in gains), § 314.742 (tax on excess passive income); Ore. Rev. Stat. § 317.090 (minimum tax).

38. Pa. Stat. Ann. tit. 72, § 7301(s.2); Pa. Stat. Ann. tit. 72, § 7301(n.1) (QSub status); Pa. Stat. Ann. tit. 72, § 7307.8 (S corporation not subject to income tax with the exception of the built-in gains tax); Pa. Stat. Ann. tit. 72, § 7602 (capital stock/franchise tax).

39. R.I. Gen. Laws § 44-11-2(d) (follow federal S election); R.I. Reg. CT 98-13 (QSub status); R.I. Gen. Laws §44-11-2(e) (minimum tax); R.I. Gen. Laws § 44-12-1 (franchise tax)—repealed by L. 2014, c. 145, Art. 12 § 20.

40. S.C. Code Ann. § 12-20-10(3), § 12-20-10(4), § 12-6-590(A) & (B), § 12-6-4430(A), § 12-6-4910(3), § 12-8-590(A), S.C. Code Ann. § 12-20-50 (corporate license tax); South Carolina Revenue Procedure No. 98-1 (federal QSub election followed).

41. Tenn. Code Ann. § 67-4-2006(a)(2) (corporation with federal S election subject to excise tax); § 67-4-2007(e) (excise tax filing obligation without regard to federal status—QSub filing obligation).

42. Tex. Tax Code Ann. § 171.001(a) (Texas franchise margin tax).

43. Utah Code Ann. § 59-7-701 (generally exempt); Utah Admin. R. R865-9I-55 (federal QSub election followed).

44. Vt. Stat. Ann. tit. 32, § 5910(a)(6) (follow federal S election); Vt. Stat. Ann. tit. 32, § 5911(a) (S corporation generally exempt); Vt. Stat. Ann. tit. 32, § 5824 (general conformity statute—provides authority to follow federal QSub election).

45. Va. Code Ann. § 58.1-401(4) (general exemption for S corporation).

46. Wash. Rev. Code § 82.04.220, § 82.04.030, § 23B-01.530, § 23B.01.550.

47. W. Va. Code § 11-24-5(d) (corporations with a federal S election are exempt from all corporate income tax); W. Va. Code § 11-24-3 (conformity provision); 5(d), W. Va. Code § 11-23-1 (franchise tax).

48. Wis. Stat. § 71.34(1)-(2) (federal S election effective, subject to ability to elect out); Wis. Stat., Wis. Stat. § 71.365(7) (federal QSub election generally followed); Wis. Stat. § 71.35 (built-in gains tax); Wis. Stat. § 77.93(1) (economic development surcharge).

49. Wyo. Stat. § 17-16-1630 (license tax).

Chapter 4

Valuing S Corporation ESOP Companies

Kathryn F. Aschwald and Donna J. Walker

S ince 1998, corporations with employee stock ownership plans (ESOPs) have been eligible to elect S corporation status, and existing S corporations have been eligible to form ESOPs, without nullifying the S corporation election. For 100% ESOP-owned companies, this change in the tax laws effectively eliminates federal income taxation. For companies that are less than 100% ESOP-owned, that portion of the income attributable to the ESOP's ownership is not taxable. For example, if an ESOP owns 35% of a company, then 35% of the company's income would not be taxable. The remaining 65% of the company's income would be taxable to the other shareholders at the shareholder level.

The elimination of taxes (completely for 100% ESOP-owned companies and partially for less than 100% ESOP-owned companies) presents some interesting valuation questions. Within the appraisal community, there long have been heated discussions regarding the appropriate methodologies to employ in valuing S corporations relative to C corporations due to their unique tax status. Thus, to a certain degree, the question of appropriate methodologies to employ in valuing S corporation ESOPs is not a new one. However, the ESOP's ability to completely eliminate taxes in some instances introduces a factor to be considered that is not present in C corporations.

The debate concerning valuation in ESOP S corporations (and all S corporations) is more specifically focused on the income approach (valuing companies based on a discounted value of future earnings) and the valuation of minority interests (how much less buyers should pay for a less-than-control interest), particularly minority interests of companies that are making distributions significantly above those necessary to meet shareholders' tax liabilities.

The income approach issue, as we will discuss below, revolves around whether the tax shield provided by the ESOP creates additional future income compared to what would occur if the company were a C corporation. If so, how much should this additional income be counted in assessing value? This issue must be addressed within the context of the use of the cash tax savings by the corporation, i.e. whether the savings are paid out to shareholders, reinvested in the company, or used to honor growing ESOP repurchase obligations.

The minority interest issue is somewhat more complicated. A minority interest is generally worth less than its pro rata portion of the 100% equity value of the company. This is because such an interest lacks control and lacks marketability. However, if such an interest receives significant interim returns in the form of dividends, then the receipt of such income returns tends to mitigate the minority interest's lack of control and lack of marketability. Investors receiving a sufficient income return on an investment are more indifferent to their lack of control and are less concerned about the investment's lack of marketability. The investor is not dependent on selling the investment in order to realize a return. The capital gains portion of the value is less than if the company reinvested the dividends, but the income portion is greater. Such a minority interest will have lower discounts for lack of control and lack of marketability, and thus, its fair market value may be much closer to its pro rata portion of the company's 100% equity value than a similar minority interest not receiving dividends or receiving dividends sufficient only to meet the owner's tax obligations. The fair market value of such a minority interest will never equal its pro rata portion of the 100% value, because the interest does not have the ability to declare dividends. Therefore, it is at risk that dividends may be reduced or completely curtailed.

Impact of S Corporation Election on ESOP Company Cash Flows

Less Than 100% ESOP

In this case, the cash savings to the company are limited because cash payments are generally made to all shareholders so that the non-ESOP shareholders have cash available to pay taxes on the S corporation income attributable to the non-ESOP shareholders at the shareholder level.

The distributions made to meet these personal tax obligations go, in the case of the non-ESOP shareholders, directly to the shareholder, and, in the case of the ESOP, to the ESOP trust. In fact, in many instances, the distributions made to meet personal tax obligations are often a higher percentage of pretax income than the combined corporate federal and state income tax effective tax rates. In either case, the cash is no longer available to the company to reinvest into productive assets. To the extent that these distributions can be used by the ESOP to pay principal and interest (in the case of a leveraged ESOP) or to pay ESOP benefit distributions, then there is a cash savings to the extent that distributions result in lower company contributions to the ESOP.

100% ESOP

In an S corporation that is 100% owned by an ESOP, there are no corporate federal income (and often state) taxes paid. Therefore, the company realizes, on an annual basis, a cash savings equal to the dollar amount of the taxes the company would have to pay were it a C corporation.

Appraisal Methodologies

The Internal Revenue Service (IRS) and the U.S. Department of Labor (DOL) generally govern appraisals for ESOP purposes. In this chapter, we will not discuss appraisal methodologies as they apply to ESOPs in general, but rather how they apply to ESOP S corporations specifically.

Value Enhancement Associated with S Corporation Election

There is no question that the absence of taxes represents true cash savings to a company. It follows, then, that the cash savings should translate into some form of enhanced value.

From the most global perspective, value is enhanced via the increase in cash flows available to the company. The source of these cash flows is the cash that would otherwise have gone to pay corporate federal income taxes. As discussed above, the magnitude of the savings depends on the percentage of the company owned by the ESOP. This value enhancement is realized in one of two ways: either through reinvestment of cash flows (in the form of productive assets or to honor repurchase obligations) or through the payment of regular dividends. The reinvestment of the added cash flows into productive assets earning a return in excess of the company's cost of capital enhances value over time as those assets become productive and generate additional cash flows and higher levels of growth than would otherwise be the case. However, when the added cash flows are used to honor repurchase obligations, the cash does not earn a return; rather, it honors an obligation that would have otherwise likely caused the company to defer reinvestment of funds into value enhancing opportunities noted above. When the cash flows are paid out in the form of dividends, the owner of the ESOP common stock earns a portion of its total return in the form of dividends. In this case, the value is captured either in a capitalization of dividends approach or in the increased marketability (or conversely lower marketability discount) of the security due to its higher income return. The capital gains portion of the value is less than if the company reinvested the added cash flows, but the income portion is higher.

If the company merely retains the added cash flows in the form of cash and marketable securities, which do not earn a return in excess of the company's cost of capital, the S corporation election may not be value enhancing. *The mere avoidance of taxes does not enhance value. The cash savings associated with the S corporation status must be put to productive use or replace the use of funds to honor obligations such as repurchase obligations that would otherwise be reinvested into productive assets.*

Initial Transactions and Updates

Standard of Value. A significant governing factor in considering the most appropriate appraisal methodologies is the standard of value for ESOP appraisals. IRS regulations, proposed regulations by the DOL, and general case law dictate that the appropriate standard of value is fair market value. Fair market value is defined as follows:

> Fair market value is considered to represent a value at which a willing seller and willing buyer, both being informed of the relevant facts about the business, could reasonably conduct a transaction, neither person acting under compulsion to do so.

Appropriate Methodologies Within the Context of Fair Market Value. The appropriate standard of value and the definition of fair market value require an appraisal incorporating the concept of "any willing buyer" and "any willing seller." For the ESOP company to retain its S election (and the associated tax savings), it must be purchased by an S corporation. The presumption of an S corporation buyer violates the fair market value standard because another S corporation is a specific buyer. It follows, then, that for annual update and transaction purposes, the S corporation is appropriately valued using capital market rates of returns developed from publicly traded C corporations. It is not appropriate to do the following:

1. Apply after-tax multiples to pretax numbers.

2. Add the present value of the tax savings associated with the S corporation election.

3. Apply after-tax discount rates to pretax cash flows.

It is extremely important to recognize, however, that this does not mean that there will not be added value associated with the S corporation status. The value of the S corporation election is realized over time as the cash flows are reinvested and the company's earnings are higher and/or growing faster than if the company were a C corporation. Intuitively this makes sense. "Any willing buyer" would naturally pay for value enhancements resulting from the reinvestment of cash flows into income-producing assets that were already in place earning a return. Those value enhancements or assets are transferable to "any willing buyer." It also follows, then, that there is no *immediate* "value pick-up" associated with S corporation status.

As a result, in an initial transaction, the ESOP should generally not pay for value enhancements that are not already in place.[1] Nor should an ESOP pay for benefits that it brings to the table (such as the S election). As discussed above, when the added cash flows are paid out in the form of dividends, the enhanced value is captured in the increased liquidity (and thus the application of a lower discount for lack of marketability) associated with closely held paying securities.

---

1. It may be, under certain circumstances, appropriate for an ESOP to pay some sort of premium to induce shareholders to sell in order to attain the 100% ESOP S corporation status and resulting enhanced cash flows.

To the extent large cash balances are developed over time, value may even be enhanced from an acquisition standpoint for those ESOP S corporations that simply hold their added cash flows. It is not likely that this value fully transfers to a minority shareholder, and to the extent it does transfer, it certainly is less than dollar-for-dollar.

Some argue that there is a significant amount of economic value associated with the S corporation election for ESOP companies, and that this economic value is equal to the present value of (or a multiple of) the future tax savings as a result of the S corporation election. Again, however, one must recognize that to retain this economic value, another S corporation must purchase the company and maintain the ESOP to keep the tax savings. Because there are fewer S corporations than C corporations, the likelihood of an available S corporation buyer is less. Therefore, within the context of fair market value, the presumption of an S corporation buyer requires the assumption of reduced liquidity resulting from a reduced number of "willing buyers." This reduced liquidity and resulting higher discount for lack of marketability would likely offset the added value implied by the present value of the tax savings to a large (if not total) extent. In addition, many other taxes (such as the LIFO recapture tax, and the built-in capital gains tax, which will be discussed later) may in fact be due from an S corporation upon sale of the company and/or upon conversion to an S corporation. These taxes would offset any value attributable to the tax savings calculated in this way.

Taking this concept one step further, one merely needs to consider the theory from a market perspective. Valuing the tax savings implicitly as described above presumes that a buyer of the S corporation would apply a multiple to pretax income. Assuming a 40% tax rate, a multiple of 5, and $100 pretax income, this implies a significantly higher price for the S corporation, as shown in table 4-1.

Table 4-1. Applying a multiple to pretax income		
	S corporation	C corporation
Pretax income	$100	$100
Corporate taxes	$ 0	$ 40
Net income	$100	$60
Times 5.0 multiple	x5	x5
Value	$500	$300

The question is, would any "willing buyer" (or any buyer) pay 67% more ($500 versus $300) for an S corporation relative to a C corporation? We believe the answer to this question is no. To a C corporation buyer, the S status of the selling company would be of no value. If the buyer were an individual, it would be more economical for that buyer to buy a C corporation and convert it to an S corporation. The cost of doing so would be much less than a 67% greater price for the S corporation. Such an individual may be willing to pay a premium for an S corporation but no more than the cost of converting a C corporation to an S corporation. If the buyer were an existing S corporation, it would not pay for tax benefits it already had.

Sale of Company and/or ESOP Termination

We stated above that in an initial transaction, the ESOP should not pay for value enhancements that are not already in place, nor should it pay for benefits that it brings to the table such as the tax-free status in an S election. However, when the ESOP is selling its position, it may be appropriate for the ESOP trustee to consider the favorable S corporation tax treatment.

When an ESOP is selling its position or being terminated, the standard of value is still fair market value. However, the financial advisor to the ESOP trustee is often asked to determine whether the transaction is fair to the ESOP from a financial point of view. This is generally interpreted to mean that the transaction must be fair to the ESOP in both absolute terms (not less than fair market value) and relative terms when compared to many financial factors that are not necessarily part of fair market value. For example, is the consideration being received by the ESOP the same as other transaction participants? If the ESOP is leveraged with debt outstanding, we look to see whether or not the ESOP's return on investment would be higher if it did not sell and simply held its investment until the debt was paid down. When the ESOP is considering a sale of its interest, then the trustee must determine that the sale is in the best interests of the ESOP participants. Therefore, a careful analysis of financial factors in addition to fair market value may include an analysis of the enhanced cash flow enjoyed by an S corporation ESOP. This is referred to by some as the ESOP's "economic value." It is typically defined as the present value of the ESOP's pro rata portion of expected corporate income tax savings under an S election discounted at an equity-required rate of return. Some assume that fair market value will be below economic value. This may not always be the case and may require consideration of financial factors other than the present value of expected corporate income tax savings.

The question is then whether the ESOP can sell at fair market value and thus below economic value. Arguably, an ESOP trustee would have difficulty accepting a fair market value buyout price if the economic value was considerably higher and no compelling reasons for a sale existed. This is most likely with a 100% ESOP-owned S corporation. In other words, an ESOP owning 100% of an S corporation may have a hold position, due to cash flows that are 100% free of corporate income taxes, that is more valuable than the price that a financial buyer or even a strategic buyer may be willing to pay. Absent compelling factors such as poor or deteriorating industry conditions or a repurchase obligation greater than the tax savings and/or outstripping the liquidity abilities of the company, there may be no reason for the ESOP to forgo its enhanced expected future cash flows if its return on investment is higher under a hold position than if it sells its ownership position. In terms of financial fairness, this seems entirely appropriate. It would be unfair to the ESOP to sell if it resulted in a return on investment below the return available to participants if the company continued on a stand-alone basis.

However, the discrepancy between fair market value and economic value as described above may be greatly overstated. First, the calculation of economic value must include all tax impacts. There are costs to converting to an S corporation as well as tax savings. These include LIFO recapture taxes and costs relating to the write-off of deferred tax assets and liabilities. Based on the experience of some of our ESOP clients who have converted from C to S corporate status, the break-even period may be two to three years. In some instances, particularly for professional service firms, the break-even period can be substantially longer for accounts receivable recapture. In addition, S corporations may be taxed on excessive passive income (over 25% of revenues) carried over from prior C corporation status. Finally, S corporations are subject to a built-in gains tax on disposition of appreciated property carried over from the prior C corporation. Also, some consideration must be given to possible changes in tax laws that eliminate the tax advantages of S corporations.

These costs may (most likely in the first years after the conversion), when factored in with the tax savings, reduce "economic value" and the relative difference to fair market value. Assuming over time the productive deployment of enhanced cash flows, the value of the S corporation will increase. As stated above, a third party should be willing to pay for this value because it is reflective of productive assets, not a tax status, and because it is transferable to a third party. Thus, over time, fair market value and economic value should converge, and "economic value" should be reflected in the price offered by a prospective buyer.

In conclusion, we urge caution in analyzing the concept of "economic value" as it pertains to S corporation ESOPs. While there may be some intuitive appeal to the concept, economic value is difficult to determine because it is affected by many variables:

- Passage of time since conversion to S corporation status
- The level of distributions
- Subsequent investment returns
- Expected tax rates in the future
- Expected holding period of investment
- Expected sale price of investments at the end of the hold period

At a minimum, it must be considered within the context of the factors discussed above that offset economic value, such as time since conversion and the built-in capital gains tax.

In any transaction, from a fairness perspective, the question of whether or not the shareholder is being adequately compensated for his or her investment, given the terms of the transaction, is addressed. The 100% ESOP S corporation situation is no different. From this viewpoint, the analysis becomes a hold-versus-sell decision. As such, factors to be considered include a comparison of fair market value as a going concern compared to the proposed transaction price, the expected return if the ESOP holds its investment, the expected return if the ESOP sells its investment, and the risk factors that would tend to offset economic value.

Conclusion

No increase in value is appropriate in the appraisal of S corporation ESOPs only as a result of a change in tax status. It is not appropriate to add the present value of the tax benefits. The appropriate standard of value and the definition of fair market value require an appraisal incorporating the concept of "any willing buyer" and "any willing seller." For the ESOP company to retain its S election (and the associated tax savings), it must be purchased by an S corporation or individuals eligible to elect S corporate status. The presumption of an S corporation buyer violates the fair market value standard because another S corporation is a specific buyer. It follows, then, that for annual update and transaction purposes, the S corporation is appropriately valued using capital market data developed from C corporations. Having said this, it is important to note that this does not necessarily mean that one is required to value the company in the market approach using imputed corporate tax rates. There are many widely accepted methodologies within the market approaches to value that use pretax fundamentals to develop indicated values; these are perhaps the most appropriate methodologies for 100% ESOP-owned S corporations. Pretax methodologies within the income approach are more problematic and beyond the scope of this chapter.

The ESOP generally should not pay for the S corporation status at an initial transaction or for update purposes. However, consideration of the enhanced cash flows resulting from the S corporation status that have not yet been invested into productive assets may be appropriate as a part of the consideration of overall fairness when the ESOP is selling its ownership position or being terminated.

Chapter 5

Administrative Issues for S Corporations

Barbara M. Clough

S corporation ESOPs are faced with unique administration challenges. The Internal Revenue Code ("Code") Section 409(p) anti-abuse test always looms over the plan sponsor's head because the consequences of failure are draconian. However, many of the standard compliance tests and issues can also be problematic for plan sponsors.

Contribution and Allocation Limits

Plan design is critical to avoid compliance problems and headaches. Code Section 404 provides a maximum deductible contribution limit equal to 25% of eligible compensation. Principal and interest payments on an ESOP note are considered employer contributions and must be included in the maximum deductible contribution calculation. Unlike C corporations, an S corporation must count interest payments when applying this limitation.

The amount of the employer contribution, whether it be in cash or payments toward the acquisition loan, can affect the Code Section 415 test. The annual additions test compares the allocations made to an individual participant to an annual limit that is indexed ($52,000 for 2014). The annual additions consist of employee 401(k) deferrals, employee Roth deferrals, employer matching contributions, employer discretionary profit sharing contributions, forfeiture reallocations, ESOP cash contributions, and shares released from encumbrance based on the lesser of the principal and interest payments or (if the plan so provides) the fair market value of the shares released. Depending upon the terms of the plan, annual addition corrections may occur either by first refunding 401(k) deferrals and other allocations in the 401(k) plan or by correcting within the ESOP by a reallocation to the extent necessary to avoid an excess by limiting and reallocating to all other eligible participants. As you can imagine, sometimes this reallocation requires several iterations and reiterations to reach a point where no participants have excess annual additions. The result of such an allocation methodology is that the ESOP benefit level is now "lumpy," meaning that those participants who were limited have smaller allocations as a percentage of pay compared to those who received additional allocations. This can be difficult for a plan sponsor to communicate to employees, especially in industries where employees share personal information.

S Corporation Distributions

Distributions of S corporation earnings can also create complexities in administration. S corporation distributions are allocated on two bases: (1) allocated shares (shares that have been released from encumbrance, nonleveraged shares, or direct purchase shares earmarked for individual participant accounts) or (2) unallocated shares (shares that are encumbered by an acquisition note and awaiting future release). When S corporation distributions (essentially dividends) are used for debt payment, the shares must first follow the tranche to which they are related. For example, assume the following breakdown of shares:

Nonleveraged	30,000 shares
Leveraged note 1	19,000 shares
Leveraged note 2	51,000 shares
Total	100,000 shares

If the plan sponsor pays an S corporation distribution, it must follow the shares. Accordingly, in this example 30% of the distribution would be allocated to the nonleveraged shares, 19% to the shares from leveraged note 1, and 51% to the shares from leveraged note 2. Only those distributions relative to any given note may be used for debt service for that note. Distributions on nonleveraged shares may not be used for note payments and must remain in the trust as cash or other investments.

Once the breakdown of the distribution has been determined it must be further broken down to determine the methodology for the allocation. Typically, distributions on allocated shares are based upon share balances and distributions on unallocated shares are based on eligible compensation, essentially allocated in the same manner as the employer contribution.

Additionally, allocations attributable to distributions on allocated shares must pass the "fair value rule." This rule requires that the number of shares allocated to the participant's account must be at least equal in value to the cash the participant would have received if the distribution had remained in cash in the plan. In the event there is a shortfall in the amount allocated, plan sponsors may use shares that have been released on unallocated shares to cover the shortfall. Additionally a special cash contribution may be made; however, this can create additional problems in conjunction with the Section 404 limits on the deductibility of contributions.

This particular problem seems to be prevalent in mature ESOPs where most of the shares are allocated or alternatively in newer ESOPs where the value of the shares is still depressed due to the outstanding debt. Careful planning and projections when S corporation distributions are used for note payments is prudent.

Share Release Calculations

Share release calculations can be extremely problematic for both C and S corporation ESOPs. The Department of Labor has as one of its initiatives an audit of ESOPs. During the investigation, the DOL will review share release calculations and ensure that the methodology used for release matches the terms of the plan documents. An important consideration is the method used to release shares: plan sponsors may use the principal-only method of release only with loans with terms not exceeding 10 years. Lengthier loans require the principal-and-interest release method.

It is important to ensure that the interest rate used in the calculations matches the rate defined in the ESOP note. Plan sponsors often confuse the interest rate on the ESOP note with that of the external note. It is important to ensure that payments match the terms of the note. For example, if the external note is with a bank or other lending institution and it provides monthly statements summarizing the required principal and interest payments, these may not be the required payment amounts for the internal ESOP note. Additionally, ESOP note documents specify the number of days that should be used in the interest calculation. The two options are calculation of interest based on a 360-day year (essentially, each month has 30 days) or a 365/366 day year (this method adjusts interest for leap years). Also included in the ESOP documents is language for determining the number of days. Many documents stipulate that the first day of the payment period is excluded, but the last day is included. It is critical to calculate interest according to the terms because DOL representatives find mathematical errors in approximately half of the plans they review.

Another area to review is how prepayments are applied; many options exist. Plans can re-amortize the remaining principal so that the note always has the same final payment date; other notes require that additional payments are counted as principal and reduce the term of the note. Other options and combinations exist; the important thing is understanding how your plan is designed and ensuring that necessary adjustments are made. Whenever payments are made in advance, it is necessary to create a new amortization schedule to calculate future interest amounts for share release calculation purposes.

The 409(p) Anti-Abuse Test

The most common administrative concern for S corporation ESOPs is the Section 409(p) anti-abuse test. Most plan sponsors think that this test is only an issue for smaller ESOPs, but the reality is that this is not true. ESOPs of all sizes and ownership percentages can be affected by the 409(p) test. Generally the abuse is not intentional but more a function of the plan's administration, other provisions set forth in the plan, or synthetic equity. It is critical that plan sponsors carefully monitor the anti-abuse tests and ensure that any changes to ownership, synthetic equity, or other plan provisions that affect account balances be considered and tested before implementation.

Generally, very small ESOPs can be the victim of 409(p) problems. Plans with only a few participants can easily have allocations that create disqualified persons (DQPs). Think of a 100% dividend distributed among less than 10 employees; many employees would likely become

DQPs, and the plan would potentially fail the nonallocation year test. Remember that failure of the nonallocation year test has no correction, and penalties for failing are draconian for participants, the plan sponsor, and the ESOP!

Small plans with a slightly greater population may pass the 409(p) test due to greater dilution of ownership; however, it is important to carefully analyze such ownership and family relationships. Synthetic equity often adds a wrinkle to these types of situations. When synthetic equity is dollar-based, such as deferred compensation agreements, the "cash" must be converted to stock based upon the current year's market value for the stock. When the stock's market value is depressed due to acquisition indebtedness, the number of shares of synthetic equity may create unintended DQPs.

Another twist on the 409(p) test is to consider a large ESOP with over 1,000 participants; one would think that a plan such as this could not have 409(p) worries. Typically that would be true. However, add the synthetic equity twist and, lo and behold, problems may arise. Think of a 100% ESOP structured with a large number of warrants to protect the selling shareholder's investment and compensate him or her for holding the note for the debt. Say that the warrants are equal to about 95% of the total number of shares of stock in the ESOP. Even if the selling shareholder has no ownership within the ESOP, the warrants must be included in part one of the test, the determination of DQPs. In this example, the individual with warrants is a DQP, with the warrant being equal to roughly 49.5% of the sum of the ESOP shares and the shares represented by the warrant.

It would be extremely easy in a case such as this to reach a 50% ownership level and thus for the plan to fail the nonallocation year test and be subject to penalties and plan disqualification. One way would be for a family member of the DQP to be hired and receive shares of stock within the ESOP, thus, under the family aggregation rules, bringing the DQP's 49.5% up to 50% or more of the sum of all outstanding shares and the shares represented by the warrant. Alternatively, distributions could be made in the form of stock and then repurchased and retired to treasury by the company, or shares would be directly sold from the ESOP to the company and then retired to treasury, in either case reducing the number of outstanding shares to the point where the DQP's percentage of equity under the nonallocation year test rose to 50% or more.

Conclusion

As you can imagine, any slight change to the design and administration of the plan can affect the testing and results. It is important to carefully review any changes with all service providers and discuss the results and implications of changes before adoption. ESOP administration can be tricky. ESOPs are like snowflakes; no two are exactly alike, and the specifics of each allocation and test can greatly vary.

Chapter 6

Complying with the Section 409(p) Anti-Abuse Rules

Carolyn F. Zimmerman
Revised by Barbara M. Clough and Thomas Roback, Jr.

Shortly after the law changed to legitimize S corporation ESOPs, it became evident that the S corporation setup was vulnerable to tax avoidance schemes of such magnitude as to render the S corporation ESOP more of a tax shelter than a qualified retirement plan. With the passage of the Economic Growth and Tax Relief Reconciliation Act of 2001 (EGTRRA), the Internal Revenue Service (IRS) moved to block those schemes. The IRS holds that the intention of any ESOP must be to spread the beneficial ownership of company stock throughout the company's employee base in a fair manner as prescribed by the Employee Retirement Income Security Act of 1974 (ERISA), *not* to benefit highly compensated and major shareholders in a disproportionate manner. To this end, as part of EGTRRA, Congress enacted Section 409(p) of the Internal Revenue Code (the "Code"),[1] which sets forth a special test that must be applied to S corporation ESOPs for them to demonstrate they are not tax shelters. Final Section 409(p) regulations are effective December 20, 2006, for plan years beginning on or after January 1, 2006.

The 409(p) anti-abuse test is quite complicated. The test requires an ESOP with S corporation stock to prove that no portion of the plan assets (or assets attributable to the plan) is accrued directly or indirectly for the benefit of a "disqualified person." The test is intended to catch abusive ESOPs, but in reality it can catch almost any S corporation ESOP. It is very important to apply the test annually and whenever there is a change in ownership, family, leverage, or synthetic equity

---

1. Unless otherwise stated, all references to section numbers in this chapter are to the Code.

programs, because a plan can fail on any day of the year. The penalties are draconian and could actually cost you your company.

History

The new law was effective immediately for S corporations that adopted ESOPs after March 14, 2001, as well as for C corporations with existing ESOPs that elected S status after that date. For S corporations with ESOPs already in existence on March 14, 2001, the law took effect for plan years beginning after December 31, 2004. Revenue Ruling 20036 clarifies which S corporation ESOPs are eligible to be "grandfathered" so as to have an effective date of plan years beginning after December 31, 2004.[2] Revenue Ruling 2004-4 addresses S corporation ESOPs set up within corporate structures that would not substantially benefit a broad base of company employees.[3]

The test described in Code Section 409(p) looks for:

1. Individual persons who own—or *could* own—more than 10% of specifically defined shares of the S corporation (see "deemed-owned shares" below), including ESOP stock.

2. Family groups, who own—or *could* own—20% or more of those shares of the S corporation. Once these people are identified and the stock of family members, including stock owned outright, has been attributed, if all their stock adds up to 50% or more of the outstanding shares of the company, the S corporation ESOP is deemed to be abusive and has incurred, or will incur, a "nonallocation year" together with the applicable penalties.

On July 21, 2003, the IRS issued Temporary Treasury Regulations Section 1.409(p)-1T, temporary and proposed regulations that actu-

---

2. Rev. Ruling 2003-6 addresses S corporation ESOPs that were hastily set up before the March 14, 2001, deadline and did not substantially benefit a broad base of employees within the S corporation. These "shells" were being offered for sale as "pre-grandfathered."

3. Rev. Ruling 2004-4 sets forth three examples of corporate structures that, according to the IRS, were not only abusive S corporation ESOPs but also "listed transactions" under Code Section 6111 (tax shelters).

ally strengthened the severity of the test by expanding the definition of "synthetic equity" (see below). These regulations are effective for plan years ending after October 20, 2003, for S corporation ESOPs that were not in existence on March 14, 2001.

Effective Date

On December 17, 2004, temporary regulations were published, applicable to plan years beginning on or after January 1, 2005.[4] However, the previous rules dealing with ownership structures that constitute an avoidance or evasion of Section 409(p), including the rules relating to structures similar to those addressed in Rev. Rul. 2004-4, apply for plan years ending on or after December 31, 2004.

There are three special "transition rules" included in these regulations:

1. ESOP shares that are held for a disqualified person before the first plan year beginning on or after January 1, 2005, will not be treated as an impermissible accrual in 2005 if the shares are disposed of before July 1, 2005 (e.g., by distribution or transfer to a non-ESOP), and no amount is contributed for the benefit of the disqualified person under any plan of the employer intended to meet the requirements of Section 401(a), including the ESOP, during the period from the first day of the first plan year beginning on or after January 1, 2005, through June 30, 2005. However, even if no amount is allocated to a disqualified person during this period, but this period is part of the first nonallocation year of the ESOP, an excise tax will apply under Code Section 4979A with respect to either ESOP shares held for a disqualified person or synthetic equity that is treated as owned under these regulations on the first day of the plan year, regardless of whether there is an impermissible accrual or impermissible allocation.

---

4. "Prohibited Allocations of Securities in an S Corporation," TD 9164 and REG-129709-03 (Temp. Treas. Reg. § 1.409(p)-1T), 69 Fed. Reg. 75455 (Dec. 17, 2004), corrected in 70 Fed. Reg. 11121 (March 8, 2005) (removing Section 1.409(p)–1T(d)(2)(iv)).

2. The 2004 person-by-person rules regarding how to determine whether a person is a disqualified person and whether a year is a nonallocation year generally do not go into effect until July 1, 2005. However, a rule excludes from the formula for determining a "disqualified person" synthetic equity that is not likely ever to be exercised (e.g., having an exercise price that is more than 200% of the fair market value of the shares on the date of grant), if that synthetic equity were to prevent a nonallocation year from occurring.

3. The 2004 rules, including those relating to the right to receive shares with disproportional voting rights (see "Synthetic Equity," below), did not go into effect until July 1, 2005, so long as there would be no prohibited allocation before then under these regulations if the 2004 rules relating to the right to receive shares with disproportional voting rights were disregarded.

The final 409(p) regulations became effective on December 20, 2006, and are applicable for plan years beginning on or after January 1, 2006. The final regulations included a number of significant differences and clarifications from the 2004 temporary regulations, such as:

- Definitions
- Reshuffling
- Treatment of deemed distributions
- Prevention measures
- Right of first refusal clarification
- Acceleration of triennial determination date
- Violation consequences

The definition of "employer" was added to the final regulations and references Treasury Regulations Section 1.410(b)-9, which defines it as the employer sponsoring the plan and all employers that are members of the controlled group of the plan sponsor. The final regulations also refined the definition of "family member" as a disqualified person only if he or she also owns deemed-owned ESOP shares or synthetic equity. Also, the provision in the previous regulations requiring attribution of ownership under Section 318 was deleted from the final regulations. The final regulations also clarified that, in determining the present value of nonqualified deferred compensation, a "reasonable" discount rate should be used.

The 2006 regulations also indicate that reshuffling, a previous correction method for a 409(p) problem, will most likely violate the nondiscriminatory requirements of Section 401(a)(4). Both the IRS and the Treasury Department support this interpretation. Nonetheless, the final regulations do not actually prohibit reshuffling.

The final regulations also added an amendment to Section 402 covering eligible rollover distributions. This amendment added deemed distributions pursuant to 409(p) to the list of payments that are not eligible rollovers. This addition extends to the proposed Roth regulations. Therefore, a deemed distribution is also not a qualified distribution from a Roth 401(k) account.

The preamble to the final regulations listed several noteworthy 409(p) prevention methods. The only preventive measure that is guaranteed to also pass muster under Section 401(a)(4) is a transfer to a non-ESOP account. More detailed requirements to facilitate this kind of transfer were also set forth, such as consistent benefit statements after the transfer, and an affirmative action taken no later than the date of the transfer (retroactive transfers are prohibited). Note that the unrelated business income tax (UBIT) will apply for this kind of transfer. Other methods are listed such as: reducing contributions for HCEs (highly compensated employees) who may become disqualified persons, expanding ESOP coverage to include all employees, providing additional benefits to NHCEs (non-highly compensated employees), or mandatory diversification of stock in the accounts of HCEs who are qualified participants under the statutory diversification provisions.

The final regulations also clarified that an individual first right of refusal to buy ESOP shares is not considered synthetic equity as long as two conditions are met:

1. The first right of refusal would not be taken into account in determining whether the S corporation has a second class of stock, and

2. The price to acquire stock under the first right of refusal is not less than the price paid to buy stock from participants pursuant to the Section 409(h) put right.

These final regulations retain the previous rules regarding calculating of the number of shares of synthetic equity that are not determined by reference to shares of stock of the S corporation. In addition, the new rules still permit the number of synthetic equity shares treated as owned on a determination date to remain constant for up to a three-year period from that date (the triennial method). However, the new rules include changes in the triennial methodology to permit the ability, during the three-year period, to accelerate a determination date prospectively in the event of a change in the plan year or any merger, consolidation, or transfer of ESOP assets under Section 414(l).

The final regulations retain the previous consequences of 409(p) failure that the ESOP fails to satisfy the requirements of Section 4975(e)(7) and is no longer considered to be an ESOP. The final regulations expand the consequences of a failure to include termination of the entity's S corporation election and disqualification of the ESOP due to operational noncompliance. The new rules also clarify that a 409(p) violation does not provide an exemption from prohibited transaction rules for exempt loans.

Definitions

In describing the 409(p) test, this chapter uses the following terms, defined specifically for our purposes:

Disqualified Person

A disqualified person is described according to the following rules:

1. *10% Individual Rule:* Anyone who holds 10% or more of the deemed-owned shares, including synthetic equity if applicable.

2. *20% Family Rule:* Anyone *and* his or her family members who together hold 20% or more of the deemed-owned shares, including synthetic equity if applicable.

3. *Special Family Member Rule:* Anyone not already described in (1) or (2) above who holds any amount of deemed-owned shares and is a family member of a disqualified person under the 20% family rule. "Member of the family" means, with respect to an individual:

a. the spouse of the individual

b. an ancestor or lineal descendant of the individual or individual's spouse

c. a brother or sister of the individual or individual's spouse, and any lineal descendant of the brother or sister

d. a spouse of any individual described in b or c above

The spouse of an individual who is legally separated under a decree of divorce or separate maintenance is not treated as such individual's spouse. Under Code Section 409(p), the meaning of "family member" is extremely broad and may include stepsiblings or cousins.

Deemed-Owned Shares

Deemed-owned shares include shares allocated to a participant's ESOP account balance, plus shares that will be released to that account balance from a suspense account as payments are made on an exempt loan (see "Mock Allocation" below). They also include shares on which "synthetic equity" is based if inclusion will result in the individual becoming a disqualified person. Shares owned outright are not considered to be deemed-owned shares (but will count for purposes of determining a nonallocation year—see below).

Mock Allocation

To determine the deemed-owned shares that will come from the suspense account in the future, a mock allocation is performed, using the percentage of shares to total shares as they were allocated in the most recent plan year.[5]

Prohibited Allocation

A prohibited allocation is either an *impermissible accrual* or an *impermissible allocation* made for the benefit of a disqualified person during

---

5. Although Code Section 409(p) clearly states that "mock allocation" can be calculated based on the most recent share release calculation, there is speculation in the S corporation community that the prior year's ending balances could be used.

a nonallocation year. An impermissible accrual occurs to the extent that stock of the sponsoring S corporation owned by the ESOP and any assets attributable thereto are held in the ESOP trust for the benefit of a disqualified person during a nonallocation year. "Assets" includes not only S corporation stock but also any distributions made on such stock, including earnings thereon, plus proceeds from the sale of S corporation securities held for the disqualified person in the ESOP (including earnings). The final regulations retained this provision despite concerns voiced by some members of the S corporation ESOP community.

An impermissible allocation is one that occurs directly or indirectly under any qualified plan of the employer to the extent the disqualified person accrues additional benefits under the ESOP or other qualified plan of the employer that, but for the nonallocation year, would otherwise have been added to his/her account and invested in employer securities consisting of stock in an S corporation owned by the ESOP.[6]

Synthetic Equity

Synthetic equity includes the underlying shares of any stock acquisition program, such as stock appreciation rights (SARs), incentive or other stock options, a similar right to future cash payments based on the stock value or appreciation in value, a right to acquire stock or assets of a related entity, nonqualified deferred compensation plans, phantom stock, warrants, restricted stock, a deferred issuance stock right, split-dollar life insurance, or any right the value of which is based on the value of underlying shares of company stock. Also included are all nonqualified deferred compensation programs, i.e., any right to receive compensation for services performed for the S corporation (or related entities) that is deferred beyond 2½ months after the year in which services are performed.

The 2004 regulations expand the definition of synthetic equity to include the right to acquire stock or assets of a related entity. They also exclude nonqualified deferred compensation that was taken into account before January 1, 2005, for purposes of FICA (the Federal Insurance

---

6. For a full discussion of "impermissible allocation" and "impermissible accrual," see Treas. Reg. § 1.409(p)-1T at *Federal Register*, vol. 71, no. 244, pp. 76134-45.

Contributions Act) and was outstanding before the first date on which the ESOP acquired any employer securities.

The 2004 regulations define synthetic equity as follows:

1. If a synthetic equity right includes a right to purchase or receive shares of S corporation stock that have per-share voting rights greater than the per-share voting rights of one or more shares of S corporation stock held by the ESOP, then the number of shares of deemed-owned synthetic equity attributable to such right is at least equal to the number of shares that would have the same voting rights if such shares had the same per-share voting rights as shares held by the ESOP.

2. The number of synthetic equity shares for nonqualified deferred compensation may be determined as of the first day of the ESOP's plan year, or any other reasonable determination date or dates during a plan year that is consistently used by the ESOP for this purpose for all persons. The date used must be reasonably representative of the share value of the S corporation's stock. The number of shares of synthetic equity treated as owned for any period from a determination date through the date immediately preceding the next following determination date is the number of shares treated as owned on the first day of that period.[7]

3. The third rule applies to cases in which the ESOP does not own 100% of the S corporation stock. If such is the case, the number of synthetic shares otherwise determined is reduced ratably to the

---

7. The ESOP may provide, on a reasonable and consistent basis used by the ESOP for this purpose for all persons, that the number of shares of synthetic equity treated as owned on an identified determination date remain constant for the period from that determination date until the date that immediately precedes the third anniversary of the identified determination date. As new grants are made during this three-year period, the appropriate number of shares of synthetic equity resulting from the new grant would be determined at the next determination date, which would likewise remain constant during the remainder of the same three-year period. The ESOP must recalculate the number of shares of this type of synthetic equity at least every three years, based on the S corporation share value on the applicable determination date and the aggregate present value of nonqualified deferred compensation on that determination date.

extent that shares of the S corporation are owned by a person who is not an ESOP (and subject to federal income taxes).[8]

Family Member

For the family aggregation tests, family members of an individual include the following:

1. The individual's spouse

2. An ancestor or lineal descendant of the individual or the individual's spouse

3. A brother or sister of the individual, or of the individual's spouse, *and* any lineal descendant of the brother or sister

4. The spouse of anyone in (2) or (3), such as in-laws, nieces, nephews, niece and nephew spouses, etc.

Note: The definition of "spouse" does not include those who are legally separated or divorced.

Triennial Recalculations

The test under Section 409(p) must be performed no less frequently than annually; however, if the terms of the ESOP so provide, synthetic equity may be redetermined not less frequently than every three years. Accordingly, a plan document may "fix" the number of shares of synthetic equity for a specified period beginning on the determination date and ending not later than the third anniversary of the identified determination date. It should be noted that additional accruals, allocations, or grants of synthetic equity that are made during the triennial period must be taken into account on each determination date within the period. Once a triennial determination date is set, it can be changed

---

8. For example, if an S corporation has 200 outstanding shares, of which Bob owns 50 shares and the ESOP owns the other 150 shares, and Susie would be treated as owning 200 synthetic equity shares if the ESOP owned 100% of the S corporation shares, the number of synthetic shares treated as owned by Susie is decreased from 200 to 150 (because the ESOP owns only 75% of the outstanding stock of the C corporation rather than 100%).

only through a plan amendment and must be earlier than the original triennial determination date; i.e., the date cannot be extended.

Nonallocation Year

A nonallocation year is any plan year in which disqualified persons own (or are deemed to own) at least 50% of the stock of the S corporation or at least 50% of the outstanding shares of stock in the S corporation (including deemed-owned shares).

The Test

To perform the test, you will need the following information:

- ESOP participants and shares owned, both inside and outside the ESOP
- Family relationships of ESOP participants, including persons not in the ESOP
- Owners of synthetic equity, if any

The test itself consists of two parts. In Part One, the tester looks for ESOP participants who meet the criteria for disqualified persons. If there are none, there is no need to proceed any further. However, if there is even one disqualified person, the tester must proceed to Part Two to test for a nonallocation year.

Part One

In practice, Part One consists of three steps that should be performed for every person who could be a disqualified person under Section 409(p). Theoretically, this is any person who does *not* fall into the following category:

- An ESOP participant who does not now and never will own more than 10% of the ESOP shares, both allocated and unallocated, *and*
- Does not own any synthetic equity, *and*
- Is not a family member of anyone who owns shares inside or outside the ESOP, or any form of synthetic equity.

To begin Part One, the tester may set up a spreadsheet (see the appendix to this chapter) containing all ESOP participants and owners of synthetic equity, showing the following:

- ESOP allocated stock
- ESOP "mock allocation" (participant's portion of the unallocated stock)
- Synthetic equity holdings of everyone, together with a translation into the number of shares represented (in the case of a less-than-100% ESOP, in proportion to the ESOP's ownership percentage). Synthetic equity not based on stock is converted to a number of shares equal to the present value of the synthetic equity divided by the fair market value of the S corporation stock.
- Total deemed-owned shares belonging to each participant
- Percentage of total deemed-owned shares owned by individual
- Family relationships

Using this information, you can now determine which, if any, of these people are disqualified persons.

- Step 1: Apply the 10% Individual Rule, with and without synthetic equity.
- Step 2: Apply the 20% Family Rule, with and without synthetic equity.
- Step 3: Apply the Special Family Rule.

Note: The 2004 regulations provide that, in computing the percentages, the amount of synthetic equity shares added to the denominator of the fraction consists of only those shares owned by the person, or by the person and his or her family members.

According to the regulations, the following definition applies for determining a disqualified person:[9]

---

9.   Temp. Treas. Reg. § 1.409(p)-1T(d).

General rule. A disqualified person is any person for whom—

(i) The number of such person's deemed-owned ESOP shares of the S corporation is at least 10 percent of the number of deemed-owned ESOP shares of the S corporation;

(ii) The aggregate number of such person's deemed-owned ESOP shares and synthetic equity shares of the S corporation is at least 10 percent of the sum of:

(A) The total number of deemed-owned ESOP shares, and

(B) The person's synthetic equity shares of the S corporation.

(iii) The aggregate number of deemed-owned ESOP shares of such person and of the members of such person's family is at least 20 percent of the number of deemed-owned ESOP shares of the S corporation; or

(iv) The aggregate number of the S corporation's deemed-owned ESOP shares and synthetic equity shares of such person and of the members of such person's family is at least 20 percent of the sum of:

(A) The total number of deemed-owned ESOP shares, and

(B) The synthetic equity shares of the S corporation owned by such person and the members of such person's family.

Part Two

After determining which persons are disqualified persons under the rule, calculate the aggregate ownership of all disqualified persons. Include shares owned outright and apply family attribution rules. If the total number of shares owned by disqualified persons is 50% or more of the outstanding shares of the S corporation, including synthetic equity for only those individuals identified as disqualified persons, a nonallocation year can, or has, occurred. The temporary regulations describe a "nonallocation year" as follows:[10]

(1) *Definition generally.* A nonallocation year means a plan year of an ESOP during which, at any time, the ESOP holds any employer securities that are shares of an S corporation and either—

(i) Disqualified persons own at least 50 percent of the number of outstanding shares of stock in the S corporation (including deemed-owned ESOP shares), or

(ii) Disqualified persons own at least 50 percent of the sum of:

(A) The outstanding shares of stock in the S corporation (including deemed-owned ESOP shares), plus

(B) The shares of synthetic equity in the S corporation owned by disqualified persons.

---

10. Temp. Treas. Reg. § 1.409(p)-1T(c).

Penalties

There are two tiers of punishment waiting for an S corporation ESOP that has incurred a nonallocation year.

First, the ESOP must treat as distributable (and therefore taxable) any allocation made to the account of a disqualified person in that year.

Second, the S corporation must pay an excise tax consisting of 50% of the total amount of the funds involved, including any prohibited allocations or accruals made to disqualified persons in that year as well as the total value of synthetic equity owned by disqualified persons during that year, even if they did not receive an allocation during the year.

In the first nonallocation year of an S corporation ESOP, the tax is 50% of the total value of deemed-owned shares and synthetic equity owned by all disqualified persons, even though no prohibited allocations were made during such year.

In addition, if a prohibited allocation occurs, the plan has then failed to satisfy the requirements of Section 4975(e)(7) and ceases to be an ESOP. Should this occur, the exemption from excise tax on prohibited transactions for loans to leveraged ESOPs would cease to apply, and the employer would then owe an excise tax with respect to the outstanding securities acquisition loan(s). In addition, the plan would then be considered to have not been operated in accordance with its terms and Section 409(p) and would fail to meet the plan qualification requirements, which would then cause the corporation's S election to terminate.

Avoiding a Nonallocation Year

The safest way to avoid a nonallocation year is to perform the Section 409(p) tests well in advance of the year in question. For most companies, this will mean finding a third-party administrator who is knowledgeable enough to run the test correctly. For others, they may attempt to run the tests themselves. In any case, some person at the company should be conversant with the tests even if a third-party administrator is running them.

The correction will depend upon why the company failed Section 409(p), and by how much. The reasons for failure could have to do with existing S corporation ESOP allocations, future S corporation ESOP allocations (mock allocations or future contributions), synthetic equity, or ownership of stock outside the S corporation ESOP. Remember that a correction cannot be made to the holdings of non-disqualified persons to bring the percentage of stock owned by the disqualified persons into the passing range. Any steps taken to prevent a nonallocation year must be in accordance with the terms of the plan document as well as the nondiscrimination requirements of Code Section 401(a)(4).

It is critical to note that the nonallocation year test is an every-day test and there is no correction for a failed 409(p) test. Corrective measures must be taken before the test fails. Accordingly, any changes in stock ownership or synthetic equity must be considered and tested before implementation.

Corrections

Following is a list of solutions that may be used in avoiding a nonalloca-tion year. When considering a correction, it is extremely important to fit the solution to your particular company.

- *Amend your plan to include "fail-safe" language that would allow the plan to correct the cause of a nonallocation year in any given year.* This is not a correction in itself, but it is thought to add credibility to an S corporation ESOP plan document.

- *Amend your plan to provide more liberal eligibility and allocation requirements.* This is not a correction in itself, but it if there are more eligible participants, it will dilute the stock allocation and thereby reduce the ownership percentages.

- *Elect C corporation status.* This is the ultimate correction, which may in the end be the best one depending upon your goals for equity compensation incentives inside your company and your company's particular tax situation. Smaller companies may find that the taxes they would pay as a C corporation are considerably less than the amounts of the S corporation ESOP penalties under Code Section 401(p).

- *Pay the excise tax.* Remember that the tax must be paid in every year that has incurred a nonallocation year. This is a very expensive option, but might be worth it and should be considered.

- *Amend the plan's allocation provisions to restrict participants as needed to avoid a nonallocation year.* Some S corporation ESOPs restrict plan participants from accumulating more than 10% of the total ESOP allocations and any family group from reaching the 20% level. This may be only a partial solution, depending upon family groups within the company. Recent guidance from the IRS during the determination letter process has indicated that limiting plan participants is not the preferred methodology to avoid nonallocation years. The IRS has indicated that it will not issue determination letters for plans with corrective language of this type in the document. Additionally, the IRS has indicated that plans with limitation language must demonstrate through passing the 401(a)(4) non-discrimination test that the plan in operation is not discriminatory in nature.

- *Amend the plan to allow for in-service distributions to eliminate holdings of stock that have created disqualified persons.* This solution depends on the willingness of the plan participants to take in-service distributions. They cannot be forced into taking them. Also remember that such a provision must be nondiscriminatory. The sale must occur before a nonallocation year occurs. Analysis should occur before the sale to ensure that the sale does not result in new disqualified persons.

- *Begin profit sharing accounting ("reshuffling") to keep ESOP account balances in line with each other.* You could still have a problem if your plan is very small and 100% owned by the ESOP. However, Section 409(p) states that the test could fail at any time during the plan year, so potentially a plan could be failing 409(p) before the "reshuffling" is performed. The final regulations indicate that absent a special rule for applying the nondiscrimination requirements of Section 401(a)(4), it could be difficult to reshuffle without violating the section.

- *Transfer the S corporation securities out of the ESOP component of the plan or to another qualified plan that is not an ESOP.* Provided the plan document allows for such a transfer, all nondiscrimination requirements under Section 401(a)(4) are considered to have been passed. The transfer must be accomplished by an affirmative action taken no later than the date of the transfer, and all subsequent actions (such as participant statements) must confirm that the transfer occurred on the set date.

- *Minimize or eliminate synthetic equity programs.* Some companies have successfully replaced these programs with cash bonus plans or other plans not tied to company stock or stock performance. Remember that, according to the temporary regulations, even nonqualified deferred compensation plans are considered to be synthetic equity if not paid within 2½ months after the close of the year in which services are performed.

- *Have the company redeem and retire or recontribute ESOP shares.* This helps keep shares in the ESOP to a manageable percentage and allocates them across a broad range of participants.

- *Match 401(k) deferrals with company stock.* This increases the base of ownership within the ESOP.

- *Lower individual direct ownership levels through a sale to the ESOP or another buyer.* Consider family relationships.

The most important thing for S corporation ESOP sponsors to take into account is that the IRS is very serious about disallowing S corporation ESOPs that may not be broad-based under the definitions and requirements of Code Section 409(p). Consider what Section 409(p)(7) says:

> (A) *In general.* The Secretary shall prescribe such regulations as may be necessary to carry out the purposes of this subsection.
> (B) *Avoidance or evasion.* The Secretary may, by regulation or other guidance of general applicability, provide that a nonallocation year occurs in any case in which the principal purpose of the ownership structure of an S corporation constitutes an avoidance or evasion of this subsection.

Thus, the Secretary has the broadest powers to interpret Section 409(p) and can issue rulings as seen fit to prevent abuses. Revenue Rulings 2003-6 and 2004-4 are examples of cases in which IRS moved both appropriately and quickly to prevent abusive situations.

S corporation ESOPs must take every precaution to prevent a nonallocation year. S corporation ESOP sponsors have no choice but to take the matter seriously. To end with another quote from the temporary regulations:[11]

> (3) *Special rule for avoidance or evasion.*
>
> . . . .
>
> (ii) Under section 409(p)(7)(B), the Commissioner, in revenue rulings, notices, and other guidance published in the Internal Revenue Bulletin (see §601.601(d)(2)(ii)(*b*) of this chapter), may provide that a nonallocation year occurs in any case in which the principal purpose of the ownership structure of an S corporation constitutes an avoidance or evasion of section 409(p). *For any year that is a nonallocation year under this paragraph (c)(3), the Commissioner may treat any person as a disqualified person* [Emphasis added].

Sources

Following are some useful materials that contain analyses and examples of Section 409(p) testing.

Hector, Brian. "Legal Considerations for S Corporation ESOPs." Chapter 2 of this book.

Grussing, Bruce D., and Susan D. Lenczewski. "The Tax Free Environment of S Corporations and the Perils of the Anti-Abuse Rules." *Business Entities* 6, no. 2 (March/April 2004).

"Legal Update." *The ESOP Report* (The ESOP Association), September 2003.

Rosen, Corey. "IRS Cracks Down on ESOP S Corporation Deferred Compensation Scams." http://www.nceo.org/employee-ownership-update/2003-08-01.

Internal Revenue Service and Treasury. "Prohibited Allocations of Securities in an S Corporation" [final regulations]. *Federal Register,* December 20, 2006 (vol. 71, no. 244).

---

11. Temp. Treas. Reg. § 1.409(p)-1T (c)(3).

Appendix: Sample 409(p) Anti-Abuse Test

Disqualified Persons Determination

NAME	ALLOCATED ESOP SHARES	MOCK STOCK	SYNTHETIC EQUITY	TOTAL DEEMED-OWNED SHARES	INDIVIDUAL % WITH SYNTHETIC EQUITY	INDIVIDUAL % WITH NO SYNTHETIC EQUITY
Jack	100.00	15.00	5.50	120.50	10.31%	9.89%
Ursula	40.00	9.00	6.50	55.50	4.75%	4.21%
Gail	50.00	21.00	0.00	71.00	6.10%	6.10%
Sandy	30.00	4.00	0.00	34.00	2.92%	2.92%
Jennifer	13.00	6.00	0.00	19.00	1.63%	1.63%
Others	600.00	275.00	0.00	875.00	75.24%	75.24%
	833.00	330.00	12.00	1,175.00		

Calculate Family Percentage

NAME	ALLOCATED ESOP SHARES	MOCK STOCK	SYNTHETIC EQUITY	TOTAL DEEMED-OWNED SHARES	INDIVIDUAL % WITH SYNTHETIC EQUITY	INDIVIDUAL % WITH NO SYNTHETIC EQUITY
Jack	100.00	15.00	5.50	120.50	10.31%	9.89%
Ursula	40.00	9.00	6.50	55.50	4.75%	4.21%
Gail	50.00	21.00	0.00	71.00	6.10%	6.10%
Sandy	30.00	4.00	0.00	34.00	2.92%	2.92%
					24.08%	23.12%

Run 409(p) Test

DISQUALIFIED PERSONS	ESOP SHARES	MOCK STOCK SHARES	SYNTHETIC EQUITY	OUTRIGHT SHARES	TOTAL OWNERSHIP
Jack	100.00	15.00	5.50	200.00	320.50
Ursula	40.00	9.00	6.50	5.00	60.50
Gail	50.00	21.00	0.00	6.00	77.00
Sandy	30.00	4.00	0.00	0.00	34.00
Subtotal	220.00	49.00	12.00	211.00	492.00
Others	613.00	281.00	0.00	0.00	1,386.00

Calculation: 26.20% (492 / [492 + 1,386])

NONALLOCATION YEAR? NO

Chapter 7

Long-Term Incentive Plans in S Corporation ESOP Companies

Matthew G. Keene

No discussion about compensation in ESOP companies is complete without the topic that often provokes the most interest and yet is often the least understood: the long-term incentive plan (LTIP). This is especially true for S corporation ESOP companies, where additional complexities and considerations come into play. This chapter seeks to shed light on this topic by spotlighting the unique issues faced by S corporation ESOP companies in designing, implementing, and administering LTIPs.

This chapter covers important LTIP planning issues (such as eligibility, taxation, and accounting) but does not attempt to cover each issue in great detail unless it is particularly germane to an S corporation ESOP company. This higher-level discussion helps to keep the focus on the unique intersection of LTIPs and S corporation ESOP companies. For a more detailed discussion of many of these issues, see Paul Horn and Matt Keene, *Long-Term Incentive Plans for ESOP Companies* (Oakland, CA: NCEO, 2012).[1]

For purposes of this chapter, the term "LTIP" refers to a form of nonqualified deferred compensation arrangement used to provide cash or stock awards to participants on a tax-deferred basis. In particular, the main focus is on LTIPs used by S corporation ESOP companies to provide equity-based awards, which primarily take the form of stock appreciation rights (SARs) or phantom stock.[2]

---

1. Available at http://www.nceo.org/r/LTIPs.
2. Throughout this chapter the term "actual equity awards" is used to refer to awards that may be settled in actual shares of company stock, such as restricted

123

Purpose of LTIPs

LTIPs are used for many purposes, but most of these uses revolve around the central theme of recruiting, retaining, or rewarding a subset of executives and key employees ("recipients" hereafter). ESOP companies often note that new recruits—especially younger recruits—do not appreciate the often significant ESOP benefit because they have never experienced either the value or culture that an ESOP can foster. Companies sometimes need a benefit to bridge the annual base salary and bonus and the pay-at-separation ESOP. Enter the LTIP. LTIPs can also help to retain recipients via vesting schedules that can be the same or different than the ESOP vesting schedule. LTIP vesting schedules may even be conditioned on individual or company performance. Further, LTIPs can be customized to individual recipients to encourage and reinforce the recipient's attainment of a goal that he or she is uniquely able to accomplish for the company. Finally, LTIPs may also be used to allow recipients to defer compensation to later years when the recipient's tax rate may be lower. For these reasons and others, LTIPs provide a flexible and powerful tool to supplement the already powerful benefits of ESOPs.

Special S Corporation ESOP Company Considerations

Unique issues exist when granting any type of LTIP in an S corporation that has an ESOP.

Section 409(p)

The S corporation ESOP anti-abuse rules in Code Section 409(p) are covered in more detail in other parts of this publication, but this chapter

---

stock and stock options. The term "equity-based awards" refers to awards that are valued based on company stock but settled in cash, such as phantom stock units and stock appreciation rights. The term "synthetic equity" has special meaning under Section 409(p) of the Internal Revenue Code of 1986, as amended (the "Code"), and may refer to any of actual equity awards, equity-based awards, or even deferred cash compensation. This chapter limits the use of "synthetic equity" to this special definition under Section 409(p).

will discuss the particularly surprising consequences that may stem from implementing even a modest LTIP in the right (or wrong) situation. Section 409(p) can be a major design consideration for ESOP sponsors who are S corporations.

Tax Distributions and Tax Filing Requirements

Section 409(p) is not the only special planning consideration for S corporation ESOP companies when it comes to long-term incentives. Unlike C corporations, S corporations are pass-through entities, and shareholders are taxed on their pro-rata share of company income. A significant number of S corporation ESOP companies will end up with the ESOP owning 100% of the common stock because having a small number of shares held by individuals other than the ESOP presents various issues. S corporations also may only have one class of stock outstanding, and each share of stock must receive the same per-share distribution.

> *Example 1.* An ESOP owns 90% of an S corporation and an individual owns 10%. If the S corporation has $1,000,000 of taxable income, then 10% of this amount, or $100,000, is reported on the personal income tax return of the individual. If the individual's income tax rate is 40%, this $100,000 of ascribed income produces a $40,000 income tax liability for the individual but does not provide any cash to pay this liability. In this situation, the S corporation often makes a distribution of $40,000 to the individual for the individual to remit to the IRS. Given the ownership ratio of 10% for the individual and 90% for the ESOP, if the individual receives a $40,000 distribution, the ESOP must receive a $360,000 distribution to keep the per-share distribution rate the same. Thus, it is uncommon for S corporation ESOP companies to permanently maintain an ownership structure where the ESOP owns the vast majority of the shares and an individual or individuals own a small minority of the shares. As to LTIPs, this often prevents S corporation ESOP companies from adopting LTIPs that provide actual equity awards (e.g., restricted stock or stock options), since such awards would likely represent a small percentage of total outstanding shares.

In addition to a federal tax liability, shareholders also may owe state tax in each jurisdiction where the company performs significant business. The company may file a composite return and pay the tax for shareholders, but this adds further complexity and angst for the company's finance department. For these reasons, companies that have elected S corporation status often transition their stock option plans to equity-based plans such as SARs.

Shareholder Limitations

S corporations also are subject to limits on the number and types of shareholders. This is one reason for not adopting LTIPs in the form of actual equity awards since the total LTIP recipients, when added to those with direct ownership of shares, could exceed the 100-shareholder S corporation limit. Alternatively, the LTIP recipients might inadvertently transfer the shares to an impermissible shareholder.

For all of these reasons, most S corporations design LTIP programs to provide equity-based awards such as phantom stock or SARs that are typically paid out in cash. Equity-based awards are tied to the value of company stock but do not receive a portion of the S corporation's flow-through income, nor do they count when determining the number or type of shareholders of the S corporation.

Given the above, ESOP companies that have converted from C corporation to S corporation status may also wish to convert their LTIPs providing actual equity awards to those providing equity-based awards. Care is needed to prevent unintended consequences under Section 409A if, for example, the company moves from an award that is not subject to Section 409A (e.g., restricted stock) to one that generally is (e.g., phantom stock).

Determining LTIP Participants; ERISA Exemption

An ESOP is a tax-qualified plan that must (1) cover a certain percentage of the employer's workforce (generally a percentage of non-highly paid employees that is at least 70% of the percentage of highly paid employees covered by the plan), and (2) provide allocations to participants on a nondiscriminatory basis.[3] In contrast, an LTIP is designed to give the employer significant discretion on which recipients to cover and what level of benefit to provide to each.

An LTIP that provides benefits payable at termination of employment or beyond is considered a "pension plan" subject to all of the re-

---

3.   Code Sections 401(a)(4) and 410(b).

quirements of the Employee Retirement Income Security Act of 1974, as amended (ERISA), unless a specific exemption applies.[4] Since the LTIP as designed and operated will not comply with the ERISA requirements generally applicable to employer-sponsored retirement plans (e.g., participation, vesting, and funding), it is important that the LTIP satisfy the two rules for exemption from these ERISA requirements.

The first condition for exemption from these ERISA rules is that the LTIP be "unfunded." This means that LTIP benefits must be paid from company assets and not funded through a separate trust that is beyond the reach of company creditors.[5]

The second condition for exemption is that LTIP coverage be limited to only certain recipients, or to what is commonly referred to as a "top hat" group of employees. This is vaguely defined in ERISA Section 401(a) (1) as a "select group of management or highly compensated employees."

This "select group" phrase has never been explicitly defined, and it evades efforts to apply a clear rule of thumb. It is not atypical to see LTIPs that cover up to 10% of all employees, but this percentage often may be a bit higher in smaller companies and somewhat lower in larger companies. Since no "select group" safe harbor exists, this is clearly an area where plan sponsors should involve their legal counsel to evaluate their LTIP arrangement based on its unique facts and circumstances.[6] As noted previously, if plan coverage is not properly limited, the ERISA rules would apply, meaning the plan as designed would fail to meet the ERISA rules, which would trigger plan funding requirements that would cause participants to be immediately taxed on their vested benefits.[7]

Notwithstanding the rules discussed above, an LTIP that provides only in-service payments may not be subject to ERISA, *regardless of the number of employees covered.* This is because the relevant provisions of ERISA apply only to a "pension benefit plan," defined as a plan providing

---

4. ERISA Sections 3(2) and 3(3).
5. ERISA Sections 201(2), 401(a)(1), and 301(a)(3).
6. See Department of Labor (DOL) Advisory Opinion 90-14A, in which the DOL stated that the term "select group" refers only to those employees who, "by virtue of their position or compensation level," have the ability to negotiate the terms of their deferred compensation arrangement, and thus who do not need the substantive rights and protections afforded by ERISA."
7. Code Section 402(b).

retirement income or the deferral of income to the termination of employment or beyond. Hence, a stock option plan or any other plan that defers benefits merely for a period of years ending before termination of employment could cover a large group of employees and generally avoid being subject to ERISA.[8]

In situations where the plan sponsor wants to offer the LTIP to a broader group of LTIP recipients beyond a likely top-hat group, the mid-term arrangement discussed later under the topic of duration is an option to consider.

Equity Dilution

LTIP awards arguably can result in the dilution of company share value. Dilution can occur where actual shares under the plan are awarded or become owned by employees who do not pay fair market value for these shares. These additional outstanding shares increase the number of shares by which the company's equity value is divided and hence dilute (i.e., decrease) the resulting share value as well as earnings per share.[9]

Dilution can also occur in the case of equity-based awards like SARs or phantom stock, where there is no increase in the number of outstanding shares. The appreciation in value of these equity-based units represents a future claim on the assets of the company. Hence, this cost will be taken into account by the appraiser in determining the company's equity value.

> *Example 2.* An LTIP awards SARs at fair market value to several employees. At the end of the year the SARs have appreciated an aggregate value of $10,000. This amount would be subtracted from company enterprise value by the appraiser in determining the company's value.

---

8. Being subject to ERISA is not necessarily all bad from the employer's perspective. An LTIP that is an ERISA "top hat" plan still remains subject to certain ERISA rules. For example, state law claims (e.g., contract) against a top hat plan are preempted by ERISA, and such claims against the plan would be removed to federal court. A top hat plan must file a letter with the DOL following plan adoption, however, to be exempt from ERISA reporting requirements.

9. For S corporation ESOP companies, the impact on earnings per share is generally far less relevant than the impact on equity value and the resulting share value.

Notwithstanding the above discussion, there is an argument that properly designed LTIPs do not really dilute the company's equity value if the grant or payment of the awards is conditioned on the attainment of performance thresholds that drive share value. This makes sense because the theory behind granting LTIP awards is that they align the company and LTIP recipients and drive mutually beneficial outcomes. As noted above, the award may result in either more shares outstanding or an additional claim on corporate cash, but if there has been a corresponding increase in equity value due to the recipients' efforts (e.g., increased earnings), the net result should be neutral.

Setting the philosophical debate about dilution aside, ESOP sponsors should have the ESOP trustee review the total LTIP pool to gauge whether it excessively dilutes the ESOP's ownership. Must the ESOP trustee actually vote on or approve an LTIP grant to an individual recipient? No, because setting compensation and these benefits is a board function. Also, most independent external trustees do not want to operate at this level of detail. However, it is a generally accepted best practice to have the ESOP trustee review and approve a prospective LTIP program as a whole.

So how large must an LTIP pool be to be of concern to an ESOP trustee? A commonly expressed range—but by no means an explicit limit—for a total LTIP pool size is 10% to 15% of fully diluted equity. While this range is often portrayed as the norm, this approach, like any rule of thumb, can present problems. The first issue is distinguishing between full-value awards and appreciation-only awards. A full-value award, such as restricted stock or phantom stock, obligates the company to pay the recipient the value of one share of stock, even if no appreciation in share value occurs. In contrast, an appreciation-only award, such as a stock option or the more common stock appreciation right, only obligates the company to pay the recipient the appreciation on one share of stock between two measuring dates. These award types are covered in detail later in this chapter.

> *Example 3.* Company A has 10,000 shares of common stock outstanding and is evaluating a grant of 1,000 LTIP units to produce an LTIP pool that is roughly 10% of common stock outstanding. The LTIP award will be granted on December 31, 2014, and will vest and be paid on December 31, 2017. Assume the value of Company A stock is $10 per share on December 31, 2014, and $15 per share on December 31, 2017.

The dilutive effect differs depending on the type of award used. Since each unit of phantom stock is worth the same as a share of common stock, 1,000 phantom stock units in the above example would represent 10% of common stock (i.e., 1,000 divided by 10,000). In contrast, 1,000 SARs are only worth $5 per unit on December 31, 2017, because each SAR unit is only worth the amount of appreciation between the date of grant and the date it is paid (i.e., $15 less $10 equals $5 of appreciation per unit). The total appreciation for the SARs is $5,000 (i.e., 1,000 SAR units times $5 per unit). The total value of Company A's common stock is $150,000 (i.e., 10,000 common shares times $15 per share). Thus, in contrast to the phantom stock, the cash outlay for the SARs is only equal to about 3.3% of the value of the common stock (i.e., a $5,000 SAR liability divided by the $150,000 value of common stock).

This is a fairly typical example if the appreciation-only award has a limited timeframe (above just three years). Thus, the 10% to 15% LTIP carve-out rule of thumb needs to consider the timeframe of appreciation-based awards like SARs to ensure the SARs are not artificially limited by the notion of a "normal" LTIP pool size.

A second issue can arise when companies first set an LTIP pool size and then grant awards to individual recipients—a so-called "top-down" approach. In this case, the awards ultimately may turn out to be too rich or too lean. For example, a 10% LTIP pool going to two executives who are already at the 90th percentile for total cash compensation may be too rich, whereas a 15% LTIP pool going to 20 executives who are only at the 50th percentile on total cash compensation may be too lean. Accordingly, it is often a good idea to also use a "bottom-up" approach as a starting point in making awards.

In the bottom-up approach, the awards are built starting at the individual level considering market compensation data. For this analysis, companies should consider the value of the LTIP award and where the LTIP award will place the individual's total direct compensation (base, bonus, and LTIP) versus the desired targets. The awards are then summed for all intended recipients and also include a cushion to allow for future LTIP participants and recruiting needs.

The resulting total number of awards becomes the rough LTIP carve-out as a percentage of common stock. Of course, it is a good idea to compare this total to the 10% to 15% norm. For example, if the result of the bottom-up approach is a 25% pool, you should ask how your plan is different and why it is outside the common range. Is the pool going to a broader group of individuals? Where does it place recipients on total direct compensation versus market data? Do you have mid-term appreciation awards (e.g., awards that limit appreciation to three to five years) that should not be considered a full share of stock?

Governance

As it applies to compensation, governance refers to the general system or processes used in setting compensation and LTIP awards, both in aggregate and particularly at an individual level. A documented bottom-up approach would be an example of this governance process.

There is often a confluence and overlap of decision makers (i.e., ESOP trustees, the board of directors, and top management) at S corporation ESOP companies. With proper governance, companies hope to delineate roles and define procedures for setting compensation and LTIP awards to prevent abuses of power (such as setting one's own pay).

Unfortunately, there are no black-and-white lines that distinguish between appropriate and excessive LTIP awards, just as there are no sharp lines clearly separating reasonable and excessive compensation. Each LTIP recipient provides a unique set of skills and experiences to the company, and each has a different market value for the company (and to competitors). One way to help prove the value of individual LTIP awards and the resulting total grant levels for the overall LTIP design is to benchmark total compensation for LTIP recipients.

A detailed discussion of the compensation benchmarking process is beyond the scope of this publication, but companies can either purchase compensation data and do an in-house assessment or hire a compensation consultant. Data for base salary and bonus is fairly easy to purchase, but a compensation consultant's best help often comes through the provision of LTIP information for grant values and common designs. The NCEO's periodic surveys of executive compensation at ESOP companies are very helpful for obtaining typical LTIP grant values for top-level executives in ESOP companies.[10]

---

10. See http://www.nceo.org/r/execcomp.

Attorneys often discuss the governance process surrounding compensation, and it is similar to governance processes in many other corporate functions. The key message is this: document! The process of building LTIP awards using the bottom-up approach based on appropriate market data helps evidence a reasoned approach to compensation and helps document the board compensation committee's processes. If a company has benchmarked compensation, this process should be memorialized in the compensation committee's meeting minutes or other appropriate records. On this note, the compensation committee (or board members) approving the LTIP awards are ideally outside, independent directors.[11]

LTIP Award Types

Table 7-1 shows the major LTIP categories. Of these, most S corporation ESOP companies will use SARs or phantom stock, with a general tendency toward SARs. To be thorough, the other alternatives deserve short mention before covering SARs and phantom stock in more detail.

Table 7-1. LTIP reward types				
Actual equity		Equity-based		Non-equity incentives
Full value	Appreciation only	Full value	Appreciation only	
• Restricted stock • Restricted stock units (if stock-settled)	• Incentive stock options • Nonqualified stock options	• Phantom stock • Restricted stock units (if cash-settled)	• Stock appreciation rights (SARs)	• Deferred compensation • Excess plans • Long-term cash incentives

Actual Equity Incentives

Restricted Stock

Restricted stock is an actual stock award but, unlike other company stock, comes with certain restrictions on vesting and transfer. The restrictions

---

11. For an excellent discussion on this topic, see Stephen Magowan, "Governing the ESOP Company: Fiduciary Issues and Practical Solutions for Boards of Directors in ESOP Companies," chapter 1 in *The ESOP Company Board Handbook* (NCEO, 2009).

are typically service-based or performance-based vesting, and when the restrictions lapse the recipient is issued actual shares of company stock, thus creating shares held outside of the ESOP and subject to all of the associated S corporation considerations previously mentioned (permissible shareholder considerations, flow-through income taxation, etc.).

Unlike the case with stock options, if the stock price stays the same or goes down (but not to zero), the restricted stock will still have value when the vesting requirements are met. Since an option provides its holder with the appreciation thereon and not the value of the entire underlying stock, restricted stock awards generally are smaller than stock option grants.

Restricted stock is generally taxed to recipients as ordinary income at the time it vests unless the recipient makes a special Section 83(b) election. The employer's deduction matches the amount and timing of the participant's ordinary income taxation. The Section 83(b) election allows the recipient to include the value of the restricted stock as ordinary income upon grant (less any amounts paid) and is helpful if the recipient expects the stock to appreciate significantly before the vesting date. This is because the stock appreciation after the election will be taxed as capital gain rather than ordinary income. However, if no appreciation occurs or the recipient forfeits the stock after making the election, the recipient can deduct only amounts actually paid for the stock (subject to capital loss limitations) and cannot deduct the compensation income (or FICA) previously included in income when the election was made.

Restricted Stock Units (RSUs)

Notice that RSUs may result in actual equity or may be settled in cash. If settled in cash, RSUs are really equivalent to phantom stock. RSUs are granted with restrictions (typically vesting). Once these restrictions lapse, the recipient receives either actual stock or a cash payment of equivalent value. Stock-settled RSUs are rare in S corporation ESOP companies.

Incentive Stock Options

In contrast with restricted stock or RSUs, both incentive stock options (ISOs) and nonqualified stock options (NSOs) give employees the right to purchase shares in the future at a set price within a given period. Thus, they are appreciation-only awards. The right to exercise the options may vest immediately or over a period of years.

> *Example 4.* An option with a $15 exercise price is exercised when the price of company stock is $100 per share. This produces a gain or "spread" of $85 for the recipient. The employee could exercise the option for $15 and realize an economic gain of $85 per share. If the share price instead fell to $10, the option would be worthless ("underwater"), but the recipient would not have exercised the option and would not have lost any money.

The purchase price (also called the strike or exercise price) in the case of an ISO cannot be less than the stock's value on the day the options are granted. ISOs carry other favorable tax advantages, but also come with more restrictions, which are not covered here given their complexity and relatively low prevalence in S corporation ESOP companies. If properly structured, the gain realized upon exercise ($85 in example 4 above) is not taxed as ordinary income, though it is subject to the alternative minimum tax (AMT), even if the stock is later sold at a loss. Any appreciation in stock value after the exercise of the option may be taxed as a capital gain if the requisite holding period requirements are met.

Nonqualified Stock Options

NSOs work similar to ISOs economically. In Example 4 above, the recipient would also realize $85 of economic gain upon exercise of the NSO, though the spread realized upon exercise is taxed as ordinary income. The sale of the underlying stock at a later date may qualify for capital gain treatment for any subsequent appreciation as long as the holding period requirements are met.

Among other requirements, NSOs also need to have a strike price at least equal to the stock's value on the date the options are granted to avoid being considered a "deferred compensation arrangement" under Code Section 409A and subjected to the taxes Section 409A imposes.

Care must be taken in an S corporation that the option is not treated as a second class of stock. Under Treas. Reg. § 1.1361-1(l)(4)(iii)(B)(2), options transferred to a service provider (i.e., employee or independent contractor) will not be treated as a second class of stock so long as the value of the options is not excessive compared to the value of the services, the option is nontransferable, and the option does not have a readily ascertainable fair market value (meaning the option is not traded, which would be very rare for a privately held company).[12]

As noted above, stock options and restricted stock plans are rarely used in S corporations. Actual equity awards could cause the company to exceed the 100-shareholder limit, and/or shares could be transferred to ineligible shareholders, such as an IRA. If stock options are used, they are often designed so that the shares obtained by the recipient at exercise are immediately and automatically sold to the company to avoid creating either more or impermissible shareholders.

Also, S corporation shareholders are taxed on their proportional share of company income for the period they hold the shares.[13] If the company is highly profitable, this share of income can be significant even if the ownership percentage is small.

Non-Equity Incentives

While SARs and phantom stock do the heavy lifting for many S corporation ESOP companies, non-equity incentives can often play an important role given their many forms. For this purpose, non-equity incentive plans are defined as plans where the award is not made in the form of equity, nor is the ultimate value of the award tied to company share value.

---

12. Warrants are similar to options and are provided to selling shareholders in some ESOP transactions. A warrant is a lot like an NSO, i.e., it is a right to acquire a stock at a set price within a specified period, except that warrants are typically issued *by the company to a lender* (often selling shareholders receiving a seller note) to obtain better financing terms. Typically, warrants are issued with a subordinated debt instrument in an amount projected, at the time of exercise, to provide additional return so that the overall rate of return to the subordinated debtor is appropriate. Warrants in this context (i.e., issued to a lender) can result in a second class of stock if, under all facts and circumstances, the warrant is substantially certain to be exercised and has a strike price substantially below the fair market value of the underlying stock on the date the warrant is issued. Treas. Reg. § 1.1361-1(l)(4)(iii)(A).

13. The company will issue shareholders a Form K-1 that includes their proportional income.

As discussed in more detail later, special care must be taken with non-equity incentive plans regarding the Section 409(p) anti-abuse rules. Nearly all types of deferred incentives (even an executive's own deferred compensation) must be converted into synthetic equity units that count against the Section 409(p) limits. If company stock price plummets, the value of this deferred incentive may stay the same because it is not tied to equity value, yet this relatively constant deferred value will now be divided by a much reduced company stock price for converting the deferred incentive into a number of synthetic equity shares.

Deferred Cash Compensation

In its simplest form, a deferred cash compensation plan is not much of an incentive plan at all. A participant is allowed to defer a specified amount of cash compensation (like a bonus) until a later date, and the participant is not taxed on the forgone compensation until it is ultimately received. Such plans are really a tax-planning convenience for the participants, who typically defer these amounts (as well as earnings thereon) into retirement, at which time they hope to have a lower effective tax rate.

Code Section 409A places more restrictions on these plans than existed previously. For example, the election to defer compensation generally must be made before the year in which it is earned. Thus, an executive wanting to defer 10% of compensation for 2015 must make the election before 2015, and the election is irrevocable for all of 2015. Also, the payment date or triggering event (e.g., death or separation from service) must be specified up front in the initial deferral election, and this event also must be Section 409A-compliant. In the pre-409A era, "haircut" provisions were commonly used to accelerate the payment of a reduced amount, but this type of provision is no longer permitted.

Most deferred compensation plans add some additional twists. For example, it is common for the employer to match the participant's deferrals up to some level, and the employer matching contribution may have a vesting requirement. The participant deferrals and employer contributions may be independent of a Section 401(k) plan, or they may exist to supplement the 401(k) plan, as discussed in the following section on excess plans.

Excess Plans

Excess plans are not pure incentive plans in that they are not conditioned on employee or company performance. Instead, they exist to make selected employees whole (i.e., not de-incentivize them) by replacing benefits that are curtailed by the various dollar limits imposed on qualified retirement plans, which are indexed yearly by the IRS for increases in the cost of living.

The qualified plan limits may prevent executives from receiving a proportional benefit relative to other employees. For example, if the employer's ESOP contribution is 10% of compensation, an executive earning $300,000 will have his or her compensation capped at the Section 401(a)(17) limit ($260,000 for 2014) and will only receive a contribution of $26,000 (10% of $260,000). The additional compensation of $40,000 would have garnered a $4,000 contribution, and this $4,000 may be credited to an excess plan. As discussed earlier, these plans are generally limited to a top-hat group and will provide a benefit only if the employee exceeds one of the various qualified plan dollar limits.

The most common qualified plan limits are the above-mentioned Section 401(a)(17) limit on compensation, the Section 402(g) limit on employee's pretax elective deferrals to a 401(k) plan ($17,500 for 2014), and the Section 415(c) limit on annual additions to defined contribution plans ($52,000 for 2014).

An unfunded excess benefit plan as defined in ERISA Section 3(36) is exempt from *all* ERISA rules (see also ERISA Section 4(b)(5)). This plan need not be restricted to a top-hat group. Importantly, however, the excess benefits that can be provided are *only* those curtailed by Code Section 415, which limits the benefits payable to a participant under a defined benefit plan as well as the annual allocations made on behalf of a participant to a defined contribution plan. In contrast, a plan that makes an employee "whole" for the other qualified plan limits noted above is not considered to be an ERISA excess benefit plan. Thus, this broader excess plan must be designed as a top-hat plan.

The Code Section 415 limit deserves special mention. This limit applies to all of the defined contribution plans sponsored by an employer. For ESOP companies, this means that the employee's 401(k) deferrals, the employer's 401(k) matching contribution, employer profit-sharing contributions, and ESOP contributions all count toward one $52,000 limit for a given employee. For example, if an employee defers the full $17,500 to a 401(k) plan and receives a $7,500 match, this sums to $25,000, and only leaves $27,000 (i.e., $52,000 less $25,000) to accommodate the ESOP annual addition.

Leveraged ESOPs deserve special mention here as well. The amount that counts as a Section 415 addition may be calculated by using the lesser of the employer's contribution or the fair market value of the shares released from the suspense account for the year and allocated to employees. Please note that the ESOP plan document needs to provide for the use of this method for determining the Section 415 annual addition. This can make a tremendous difference, for example, in a leveraged ESOP when the current per-share price is below the ESOP's original per-share purchase price. This often happens following a significant shareholder buyout when the company has incurred transaction debt that suppresses the share price for a time.

> *Example 5.* Company Y formed an ESOP and loaned $1,000,000 to the ESOP to enable the ESOP to buy 100,000 shares of Company Y stock at $10 per share. The loan calls for level principal payments over 10 years. Ignoring interest, Company Y will contribute $100,000 to the ESOP each year, and the ESOP will repay the $100,000 to Company Y, thus releasing 10,000 shares from the suspense account each year. If the per-share value of Company Y stock is $3 per share in year 2, the 10,000 shares released from suspense and allocated to employees have a fair market value of $30,000. Company Y contributed $100,000 to the ESOP in year 2, so the Section 415 addition is the lower amount of $30,000 if this provision is provided for in the ESOP plan document.

As noted above, S corporation ESOP companies frequently use both SARs and phantom stock for their LTIP plans, with SARs continuing to be more popular. In many cases, however, the opposite is true when an excess plan is being used as an ESOP make-up vehicle: phantom stock is typically used. This is because phantom stock provides a full-value unit that is equivalent in value to what the executive missed by being capped in the ESOP.

Excess plans typically have the same vesting schedule as the qualified retirement plans they supplement. The payment events are often the same as well, with the added consideration of Section 409A distribution limitations.

SERPs

Supplemental executive retirement plans (SERPs) still exist, though they do not seem as popular as they once were. They are certainly less common in private companies, particularly in ESOP companies where the SERP's lack of coordination with the company stock price is often considered a drawback. SERPs have received a lot of scrutiny on Wall Street and are sometimes characterized as excessive and providing a retirement benefit for executives that is out of step with the retirement benefits provided to employees at large.

SERPs can take various forms. In a defined benefit SERP, the benefit to be paid at retirement is defined, much like a qualified defined benefit pension plan. In a defined contribution SERP, the company may make annual credits to the SERP account, and the account may be deemed to grow based on investments selected by the executive.[14] Companies often fund the future SERP liability by using a sinking fund, rabbi trust, or corporate owned life insurance (COLI).

From a taxation standpoint, the SERP represents an unfunded promise by the company to pay these benefits, and the executive is generally taxed when he or she receives payments at retirement. SERPs sometimes have vesting schedules that are longer than those found with other LTIPs since the SERP is intended to provide a retirement benefit in exchange for the executive's many years of continuous service.

Long-Term Cash Incentive Plans

For purposes of this discussion, a long-term cash incentive plan is defined as one that provides a cash award that is not tied to the value of the company's equity and is (1) earned over a period of more than one year, or (2) paid more than one year after it is earned. In other words, anything other than the typical annual bonus or annual incentive plan where the award is earned over a one-year period and paid shortly thereafter. Long-term cash incentive plans usually supplement but do not replace annual bonus or annual incentive plans.

There is tremendous variety to these plans. Sometimes companies use an annual performance measurement period (similar to an annual

---

14. In contrast to an excess plan, the SERP benefits are not based on the application of the qualified plan limits.

bonus) to determine the amount of the award, but payment of the award is deferred and subjected to either service-based or performance-based vesting. Such companies like the relative simplicity of setting an annual goal, but they also want the better governance that ostensibly comes with long-term ties.

For example, a plan may provide that the CEO is eligible for a $100,000 award if operating income is $10,000,000 or more for year 1. If operating income comes in at target, the $100,000 award is deemed to be earned, but the CEO vests in this award and it is not payable until the end of year 4. In the interim, the plan provides for clawbacks that allow the company to reduce or cancel the award if the company's financials are materially restated or other egregious events occur, such as noncompete violations or unethical behavior. In this way, the company conditions some of the CEO's compensation on continued service and encourages the CEO to not focus solely on annual outcomes.

As another example, a plan may provide that the CEO is eligible for a $100,000 award if operating income has an annual increase of 5% over a three-year period. This award is paid at the end of the three-year measurement period if the 5% hurdle rate is achieved. This type of plan rewards long-term performance and encourages long-term thinking.

There are pros and cons for every approach, whether it is a long-term cash incentive plan, an actual equity award plan, or an equity-based award plan. Multi-year goals arguably provide a strong link to long-term performance, but they can be hard to set properly. For example, just one bad year in a multi-year performance period can put such plans hopelessly underwater to the point they lose all motivational capacity. The important point is to think very carefully about the goals selected for any type of incentive plan because, given human nature, individuals focus sharply on the goals set out before them. Therefore, companies need to balance important goals and should plan to spend a lot of time on the goal-setting process.

Equity-Based Incentives

By far the most prevalent types of LTIPs used by S corporation ESOP companies are phantom stock and SARs.

Phantom stock and SARs are similar in many ways, yet they are also different. They are similar in that both typically are surrogates for the award of actual company stock. In private ESOP companies, the value of both is generally tied to the value determined annually by the independent appraiser. ESOP companies also like to use phantom stock and SARs to link recipients' outcomes with those of the ESOP shareholder without creating the above-mentioned issues involved with using actual equity.

Despite these similarities, these two forms of synthetic equity are different in several ways. First, SARs may be exempt from the Code Section 409A requirements if, among other things, the SARs are issued at fair market value. On the other hand, phantom stock is generally subject to Code Section 409A unless the value of the phantom stock units is paid to the recipient within 2½ months after the year in which they vest (the general short-term deferral exception for Section 409A). Second, SARs are always based on the appreciation of the underlying common stock between two points in time.

Phantom Stock

A phantom stock grant basically is a company's agreement to pay a recipient a future cash amount equal to the value of the "phantom" company units awarded. The units track the economic benefits of stock ownership without using actual shares. Since phantom stock is an unsecured contractual right to a future interest, under a properly designed plan a taxable event does not occur until actual payment is made.

Phantom stock typically does not require investment or confer ownership to the recipient, so no voting rights exist. Phantom stock units awarded to recipients normally reflect a current company value that will piggyback off the annual ESOP valuation and can be designed fairly simply.

In a typical phantom stock plan, the recipient is granted a number of phantom stock units, and thus the award is equal in value to the number of underlying shares of company stock.

> *Example 6.* Recipient is granted 100 phantom stock units in 2014 when the company's stock price is $10 per share. The phantom stock units vest and are settled in cash four years later in 2018 when the company's stock price is $15 per share. The phantom stock units are worth $15 each (i.e., the price of one share of common stock in 2018), or $1,500 in total. The recipient realizes

$1,500 of ordinary income in 2018 and the company receives a corresponding tax deduction at that time.

Phantom stock plans are not exempt from Code Section 409A unless they comply with the short-term deferral rule. Thus, the plan will pay the value of the phantom stock units at fixed, predetermined dates that may coincide with vesting events or separation from employment. The plan will describe certain operational details about eligibility, vesting, valuation method, form of payment, and any funding vehicle. Very often the grant or vesting of the awards is conditioned on the company and/or recipient hitting prescribed performance goals.

Phantom stock is often used as a full-value LTIP award to:

- Serve as an ESOP make-up benefit for executives who are limited in the ESOP due to various qualified plan limits.

- Retain and motivate an executive or key recruit who is close to retirement and may not have time to realize the value of an appreciation-only award.

- Retain executives and key employees during an initial ESOP transaction if cash compensation is reduced to help pay for the transaction debt.

- Used along with SARs as part of a comprehensive LTIP program to provide some retention incentive if appreciation-only awards (i.e., SARs) are underwater.

Stock Appreciation Rights (SARs)

A true SAR provides the recipient with the "right" to elect to receive the appreciation on an underlying share of stock between the date of grant and the date of exercise. SARs are always appreciation-only awards, and they usually (but not always) confer an exercise timing right to recipients.

To contrast a SAR with phantom stock, the following example repeats the fact pattern of Example 6.

Example 7. Recipient is granted 100 SAR units in 2014 when the company's stock price is $10 per share. The SARs vest and are settled in cash four years later in 2018 when the company's stock price is $15 per share. The SAR units are worth $5 each (i.e., the difference in the 2018 price less the 2014 grant price), or $500 in total in 2018. The recipient realizes $500 of ordinary income in 2018, and the company receives a corresponding tax deduction at that time. Note that one phantom stock unit under similar facts is worth $15 per unit (the full share value in 2018), whereas the SAR is only worth the post-grant appreciation amount of $5 per unit.

Unlike phantom stock, SARs are exempt from the Code Section 409A requirements if they meet the following requirements:

- The exercise price of the SAR is equal to or greater than the fair market value of the underlying stock on the date of grant.
- The number of shares subject to the SAR is fixed at the date of grant.
- The SAR does not provide an opportunity for an additional deferral of income beyond the date of exercise.

These exemption requirements, of course, influence the designs chosen by ESOP companies. Most ESOP companies do not grant discounted SARs because they want the SARs to deliver value after the period of grant, so the requirement to issue SARs at fair market value to exempt them from Section 409A was not a big game changer when Section 409A was enacted.

On the other hand, the Code Section 409A prohibition on the additional deferral of income after exercise does affect SAR designs. A true SAR allows the recipient to exercise the stock right at his or her discretion during a period of time after vesting. For example, a SAR grant may be vested in year 4 and then allow the recipient to exercise the SAR anywhere between years 5 and 10. As stated above, this type of exercisable SAR is specifically exempted from Code Section 409A, but *only* if all the income (appreciation) associated with the exercise is paid within the year of exercise.[15]

Thus, in this situation, a participant's right to time the exercise equates to a lump-sum distribution because an installment payout of the appreciation would violate the exemption from Section 409A (i.e., installment payments made in years following the year of exercise

---

15. The ability to defer payment until 2½ months following the year of vesting for plans subject to Section 409A does not apply here.

constitute an "additional deferral of income" as all amounts are not paid upon exercise). Lump-sum distributions can create corporate cash flow issues for large awards, as well as taxation issues for the recipient. Accordingly, where exercisable SARs are used, the timing and funding options should be carefully considered.

It is important to note, for this purpose, that vesting and exercisability can be de-linked. Just because a participant is vested in his or her SARs does not mean the participant must be allowed to exercise 100% of the SARs at any given time. Companies using exercisable SARs often place objective caps on amounts that may be exercised at any one time to avoid run-on-the-bank scenarios. The most common restriction placed on SAR exercisability is that only a percentage of vested SARs may be exercised in a given year.

> *Example 8.* A participant receives 100 SARs on March 1, 2015. The SARs have an exercise price of $5 per share and vest on the third anniversary of the award (March 1, 2018). While the participant has an unrestricted right to the SARs at this point, the SARs have also been designed such that in any given year the participant may only exercise 20% of the vested SARs. In 2019 the participant exercises 20 SARs (20% of the 100 vested SARs) when the per-share value is $10, resulting in a payment of $100 to the participant.

It is important to carefully design the plan if the intent is to de-link vesting and exercisability for purposes of allowing the participant to settle the SARs. As discussed above, it is common for issued SARs to include an expiration period, with 10 years from the date of grant being most common. If a participant is limited in how many SARs he or she can exercise in a given year, the plan should be designed to ensure that the participant has an opportunity to exercise all vested SARs (i.e., the SARs do not expire before he or she can complete his or her exercise rights) or have a catch-all that forces SARs to be exercised at a certain date before the expiration of the plan.

Also, if the intent is to de-link vesting and exercisability, it is important to consider the impact of FICA taxes. As discussed later, FICA is generally due upon vesting, even if the recipient has received no cash and even if the SARs cannot be exercised at vesting. If the SARs carry significant appreciation at vesting, such as SARs granted at a post-transaction price in a company incurring significant transaction debt, the per-unit appreciation created as the company de-levers may be considerable.

Although SARs that are exercisable at the discretion of the participant are not compatible with installment payouts, there are other alternatives available to a company desiring to pay the SAR appreciation in installments. One solution is simply to design the SARs within the confines of Code Section 409A, namely to include in each SAR award a determinable distribution time and form established at the time of grant, whether specified by the company or elected by the participant.

> ***Example 9.*** Assume a SAR is granted in year 1 and cliff vests in year 4. The grant agreement could allow the recipient to elect, on the date of grant, to receive the payment in three installments starting in either year 4, 6, 8, or 10. This does not allow as much leeway as an exercisable SAR, and the recipient has to make this election up front when the SAR is granted, but it does provide some flexibility.

To summarize, S corporation ESOP companies tend to use either phantom stock (full-value) or SARs, but nothing precludes a company from using both at one time so long as the resulting compensation values and ESOP dilution are reasonable and within the confines of Section 409(p). Phantom stock is more popular if used as an excess plan to make executives whole for benefits curtailed under the ESOP due to qualified plan limits. Appreciation-only plans, like SARs, provide post-grant value only if the share price increases and ESOP trustees like this linkage between recipients and the ESOP shareholder. In the author's experience and from various data sources, SARs are used roughly twice as often as phantom stock plans if an S corporation ESOP company is not specifically seeking an excess plan arrangement.

Common Planning Considerations for SARs

Given the popularity of SARs for S corporation ESOP companies, it is appropriate to discuss a common design consideration. This discussion is also relevant to phantom stock or any other LTIP based on equity, but seems especially present with appreciation-only SARs.

Most equity-based LTIP plan documents will reserve a certain number of units available for grant under the plan, and the plan usually has a stated life, with 10 years being very popular. Assume a plan reserves 10,000 SAR units, which in this example happens to be equal to 10% of common shares outstanding. If the plan has a 10-year stated life, these 10,000 units have to last for 10 years absent a special approval to increase this limit. It is absolutely possible to increase this limit, but the board of directors must meet its fiduciary duty to the shareholders if it wishes to add further dilution under the plan, and the ESOP trustee will likely wish to negotiate the extent to which the pool may be increased.

The decisions facing the company include:

- Which recipients receive the SARs now?
- How much do we reserve for new recruits or promotions?
- How long should we allow the SARs to appreciate?
- Do we grant all the awards now (at one strike price), or have multiple grants?

There are many other decision points, but these frame the crux of the issue: How can the company derive the most value out of the SAR program during the next 10 years?

Vesting is not the real issue here. Vesting terms have been trending shorter in public companies. The National Association of Stock Plan Professionals (NASPP), in conjunction with Deloitte Consulting LLP, conduct a large survey titled Domestic Stock Plan Design Survey. This survey has been conducted every so often for many years. In the 2013 version, three years was the most common vesting schedule (60% of respondents), followed by four years (30%) and five years (7%). In the author's experience, while three-year schedules are becoming more popular, ESOP companies probably use four or five years at least as often as three.

Most companies will hold back units for new recipients, so the real question is whether to grant all the units a recipient will receive up front or stagger the grants. Assuming sustained appreciation in company stock value, a recipient will normally prefer to get as many SARs up front as possible and hold them as long as possible. If company share price is volatile, however, staggered grants may be preferred to avoid granting all of the units at a high point for the share price. Also, if all of the SARs mature at one time, this produces an uptick in the repurchase obligation.

Although there are infinite possibilities, three common approaches include:

- Grant and hold
- Vest and exercise
- Vest and pay

These approaches are not defined anywhere; this categorization is used here simply to help frame big-picture differences.

The *grant-and-hold approach* seems to have fallen out of favor. In this approach, awards may vest over three to five years or possibly longer but then continue to appreciate until paid at separation or another distant event as specified in the plan document (e.g., separation from service or upon retirement age). In this approach, the awards stay outstanding for a long period of time, thus counting against the available LTIP pool and also Section 409(p) testing, yet the retention value is not high since vesting has already been satisfied and may, in fact, encourage negative behavior as employees may be incentivized to leave in order to realize the value of the awards. This may also lead to the recipient "coasting" because the award is meaningful and already earned. The payment event will likely cause a spike in the repurchase obligation since the awards have been outstanding for a long time and may coincide with separation from service, which also triggers the ESOP repurchase obligation.

Under the *vest-and-exercise approach,* the awards vest over the typical three to five years and the recipient may then choose to exercise the SARs after they are vested and before they expire.

> *Example 10.* Recipient is granted 100 SAR units in 2014 when the company's stock price is $10 per share. The SARs vest four years later in 2018 when the company's stock price is $15 per share. The terms of the SAR plan allow the recipient to elect to exercise the SAR at any point after year 4 and before year 10 when the SARs expire. Assume the recipient exercises the SAR in year 10 when the share price is $22 per share. The recipient will recognize ordinary income in year 10 for $1,200 (i.e., $22 less $10 times 100 units), and the company receives a corresponding deduction at that time.

The exercisable SAR allowed the recipient to choose the exercise date between years 5 and 10 based on the recipient's income needs and expectations of stock price value. This approach also meant that the company had to be prepared to handle this liquidity obligation at any point between years 5 and 10 absent placing limits on the portion of the SARs that the recipient could exercise in a given year. Also, these SAR units did remain outstanding until year 10 and counted against the available SAR units authorized under the plan. Companies need to consider this possibility at the outset and carefully set the number of units available under the LTIP plan, considering future needs such as recruiting or promotions.

Under the *vest-and-pay approach,* the units will often vest a bit sooner (often three years), and once the units are vested they are accompanied by a forced payment at vesting. Although vesting may be a bit shorter, the biggest difference is that the vest-and-pay approach caps the value of the award at the value once vested, and this value is slated for payment. The award is considered settled and is no longer outstanding at vesting.

> **Example 11.** Recipient is granted 100 SAR units in 2014 when the company's stock price is $10 per share. The SARs vest three years later in 2017 when the company's stock price is $14 per share. The terms of the SAR plan provide that the 100 SAR units are considered settled at the vested value of $4 per unit (i.e., $14 share price less $10 grant price), or $400 in total. These 100 SAR units are no longer considered outstanding, even though the $400 vested value of the SARs may be paid in a lump sum in 2017 or in annual installments. A common feature of the vest-and-pay approach would be to grant 100 new SAR units to the recipient in 2018 under similar terms. The 2018 SAR grant would vest in 2021 and again be settled for the difference in the 2021 and 2018 price. The vest-and-pay approach could result in multiple grants in the same 10-year life of the plan, with the difference being that some of the company's liability was settled along the way at specific intervals.

Which practice is better? Neither is better and neither is worse. It all depends on each company's goals (see table 7-2).

A key tenet of the vest-and-pay approach is that the settled LTIP awards are returned to the LTIP pool and are again available for regrant. This is referred to as an evergreen pool. ESOP trustees may not be comfortable, especially initially, with the concept of an evergreen

Table 7-2. Vest-and-pay vs. vest-and-exercise approaches		
Features	Vest and pay	Vest and exercise
Flexibility with annual grants (better forecasting of future award value over a shorter appreciation period; subsequent annual grants can be adjusted up or down)	√	
Increased retention incentives (all unexercised awards are at least partly unvested, versus long-term awards that vest and continue to appreciate)	√	
Shorter line of sight between award grant and payout	√	
Help with recruiting (easier to sell recruits on cash that is 3-5 years away versus a longer period)	√	
Smooth the repurchase obligation (award values are paid along the way versus larger back-ended payouts)	√	
Provides recipient with control over taxation timing and income needs		√
Provides enhanced linkage to long-term share value creation		√
Allows focus on longer-term goals and projects		√
Can function as a pseudo-retirement enhancement		√

SAR design. In the broad arena of LTIPs, evergreen pools are generally frowned on because they may produce more dilution than a board anticipated. For example, if a board approves a phantom stock plan that authorizes phantom stock units of up to 10% of the number of common shares outstanding, this LTIP initially produces 10% equity dilution. If these awards are settled in three years and then returned to the pool and re-granted, they would produce 20% dilution because the full-value awards have been granted and settled twice in a six-year period.

This is much less a concern for mid-term (e.g., three years) SARs, however. If SARs are granted in year 1 and settled at the end of year 4, the recipient gets three years' worth of appreciation (i.e., the difference in the share price between year 4 and year 1). If these SARs are re-granted at the end of year 4 and again vest and are settled three years later at the end of year 7, the recipient gets another three years' worth of appreciation (i.e., the difference in the share price between year 7 and year 4). In total the recipient received six years' worth of appreciation, which is exactly what the recipient would have received had the awards been granted at the end of year 1 and remained outstanding for six years until the end of year 7.

The point of this example is that with an evergreen vest-and-pay SAR, the award churns frequently, but the value delivered to the recipient—and the dilution to the ESOP—is fundamentally the same. Adding an evergreen concept to a vest-and-pay SAR design helps to avoid a new discussion with the trustee and re-authorization of LTIP units every three years, under the theory that the value delivered to the recipient is the same and the award could have been designed with a longer duration (for example, six to ten years) at the outset.

In the author's experience, vest-and-pay SARs with rolling grants are almost always performance SARs, meaning that both the initial grant and subsequent re-grants are conditioned on attaining performance goals. This is part of the thinking behind having annual grants. Also, even if the SAR plan is designed as an evergreen pool, the plan could be written to allow only one or two re-grants and/or have a maximum duration of 10 years, as an example. Such a provision avoids the process of a new discussion and authorization every three years, but does impose overall limits on the plan to allow it to be reassessed periodically.

Monetizing the LTIP

Unlike public company shares, no similar market exists for private company stock of S corporations. While the private company could have a liquidity event via an IPO or sale to a third party, these events are far from certain and their timing unknown. Thus, the private company must have a repurchase program to provide real liquidity for both actual equity and equity-based awards issued under the LTIP.

This repurchase issue can become a problem for LTIP participants where they are taxed, for example, on the full amount of their option exercise and sale to the company, but the company can pay them only in part because of an annual liquidity limit or other cash flow constraints. Actual equity awards, such as restricted stock and stock options, can present a timing mismatch because the awards are generally taxed to the recipient when vested or exercised, even if the company does not have the cash to monetize the settlement of the award.

Due to these liquidity constraints and the other issues already discussed, most LTIPs for S corporation ESOP companies are in the form of equity-based awards. The equity-based awards—namely phantom stock and SARS—are normally settled in cash, and the recipient's taxation generally matches the receipt of cash.

The burden of covering this liquidity can be significant, and this LTIP liability is in addition to the ESOP repurchase obligation. On this note, when an executive covered under both an ESOP and LTIP separates from service, it creates a true "repurchase obligation" under the ESOP because the company is required to purchase the ESOP shares. Technically the obligation to monetize the equity-based LTIP award is not a true repurchase obligation since there are no shares to be purchased, but the term "repurchase obligation" is used generically to refer to the company's total cash outlay needed to settle both the ESOP and LTIP liabilities.

ESOP companies should always include unfunded equity-based LTIP awards in any repurchase obligation studies they conduct. The equity-based LTIP liability will fluctuate with company share price just as the ESOP repurchase obligation does, yet the LTIP is sometimes ignored. This is especially important as part of any significant transaction in company stock, be it a corporate redemption, sale of significant shares to the ESOP, or an investment in the company by a third-party investor. Any transaction that affects the number and/or value of outstanding shares should consider the impact on both the ESOP and the equity-based LTIP.

Companies can take one of several strategies to finance the LTIP obligation. The LTIP is never truly "funded" because it is important that the LTIP remain an "unfunded" promise to pay benefits to prevent the LTIP recipient from being taxed on funds that have been irrevocably set aside for the recipient's ultimate receipt. This financing can take various shapes, and its manner often is based on the underlying reasons for financing.

As a preface to this discussion, note that many companies employ the pay-as-you-go approach and take cash out of current operations to pay LTIP obligations as the obligations arise. The pay-as-you-go approach allows companies to retain cash and reinvest in the business, but has the possible shortcomings of illiquidity and a lack of security for LTIP recipients, and it may not provide a direct hedging strategy against the liability.

The most straightforward reason for financing against an LTIP liability is to ensure the company has sufficient cash on hand to pay the award when owed to the executive. This helps the company communicate the value of the LTIP and should also help to foster appreciation for the LTIP among recipients. In many ways this is really the same issue and presents the same considerations as financing the ESOP repurchase obligation. The issues are magnified when it comes to providing liquidity for LTIP awards, however, because the departure of one or two key executives can trigger a significant LTIP liability, whereas the ESOP repurchase obligation is spread over the entire population of ESOP participants.

Given that most S corporation ESOP companies use phantom stock or SAR awards that are ultimately settled in cash, it can be difficult to properly hedge this liability because the company cannot really invest in its own stock to serve as a hedge. The best most companies can do on this is to set up a corporate sinking fund and invest in a suitable investment portfolio to obtain some equity growth. This corporate sinking fund is really just a notional account on the corporate balance sheet and can be used by the company for other purposes. It is not irrevocably reserved as a source of funding for the LTIP.

In another approach, companies sometimes piggyback their risk mitigation strategies to provide a source of funding for LTIP payouts. For example, a company may have a key-person insurance policy on the CEO that provides a death benefit to the company in the event of the CEO's death. This policy provides the company a cash cushion to help offset the loss of the CEO. The costs of such a loss can be considerable, including the loss of strategic direction, lost productivity, downtime to search for a new CEO, and recruitment costs for the new CEO. Since the costs of paying out all benefits owed to the CEO's beneficiaries, including the ESOP account and LTIP awards, will come at the same time as these other costs, companies will sometimes increase their key-person policies to cover the costs of the ESOP and LTIP liabilities.

A "rabbi trust" could be used to hold either sinking fund assets or the COLI policies. It provides more security for LTIP recipients because the company cannot use trust assets for general corporate purposes. The rabbi trust is available for the company's creditors in the event of insolvency; this is a necessary feature to prevent the LTIP recipients from being immediately taxed on the trust's assets.

The accounting and tax treatment for sinking fund assets or COLI policies is not altered when the sinking fund assets or COLI policies are placed in a rabbi trust, since the assets of the rabbi trust are still just assets of the corporation. Think of the rabbi trust as a wrapper that is placed around corporate assets to prevent the corporation from changing its mind about financing the LTIP obligation. The company's creditors may still attach to the assets of the rabbi trust, but the company cannot simply pull the assets out of the trust and use these for general corporate purposes.

If the assets of the trust exceed what is needed to pay the benefits under the LTIP, the rabbi trust language may allow the company to pull back assets over a certain funded percentage (e.g., assets exceeding 120% of the LTIP liabilities). This determination very much depends on facts and circumstances, but it sometimes comes into play when a rabbi trust holds COLI, for example, and receives a large death benefit.

A company should enlist the help of all of its ESOP advisors, such as those for legal, accounting, valuation, and insurance matters, in choosing a funding vehicle, because the decision is complex and each company's situation is unique.

Section 409(p) Considerations

Code Section 409(p) is covered in greater detail elsewhere in this book, so the point of the discussion in this chapter is to illustrate how a small amount of LTIP value can profoundly impact the results of this test.

To allow this discussion to stand on its own, a few Section 409(p) terms need explanation. The aim of Section 409(p) is to prevent a narrow group of individuals from receiving too much of the company's value through the ESOP or through a term specific to Section 409(p) called "synthetic equity." For this purpose, synthetic equity includes actual equity awards (e.g., restricted stock or stock options), equity-based awards (e.g., phantom stock or stock appreciation rights), and even other forms of deferred cash compensation. Accordingly, extreme care must be used in designing LTIPs so as to not run afoul of the parameters set forth in Section 409(p) and its severe consequences.

One practical impact of Section 409(p)'s ownership limitations is that some companies must pay more in currently taxable compensation because they have little or no room under this test for any type of deferred cash compensation, actual equity awards, or equity-based awards. For example, annual bonuses paid within 2½ months of the year in which they are earned are not considered synthetic equity.

In very simple terms, Section 409(p) looks to see whether "disqualified persons" own 50% or more of the "stock" of a company. The mere existence of a disqualified person is not problematic, but if these disqualified persons own 50% or more of this stock then a "nonallocation year" exists, which triggers extremely adverse tax consequences. The disqualified person is taxed on the value of his or her ESOP account as if it were distributed. The company also pays an additional 50% excise tax on that value and on the synthetic equity. Even worse, the ESOP's status as a qualified retirement plan would be in jeopardy, and an ESOP is the only qualified retirement plan that is an eligible S corporation shareholder that is exempt from the unrelated business income tax.

So who is a disqualified person under Section 409(p)? There are two ways to become a disqualified person, and as always, your family members can get you into trouble. First, if an individual owns 10% or more of the ESOP shares and synthetic equity, he or she is a disqualified person. Second, if a family group owns 20% or more of the ESOP shares and synthetic equity, they all are disqualified persons, even if each member has an interest below 10%.

Importantly, direct ownership of shares is not considered for determining disqualified person status. However, direct ownership is counted for purposes of the 50% nonallocation year test. For Section 409(p) purposes, direct ownership consists of shares owned outright by an individual (i.e., shares purchased, received by gift or inheritance, or prior awards of actual equity under an LTIP that are no longer subject to a substantial risk of forfeiture).

For counting ESOP-owned shares, ESOP shares include the individual's allocated shares as well as his or her pro-rata portion of the unallocated shares in a leveraged ESOP, which is determined on the same basis as the most recent allocation. Also, only the individual's synthetic equity is included in the denominator to prevent companies from issuing worthless synthetic equity (such as underwater options) across the board to all employees to prevent an executive from becoming a disqualified person.

The following examples illustrate how Code Section 409(p) can yield surprising results.

> ***Example 12.*** Referring to table 7-3, assume Company X is 100% owned by an ESOP and the ESOP has 10,000 shares. Employee A owns 900 ESOP shares and 500 synthetic equity units. Employee B owns 900 ESOP shares and 100 synthetic equity units. Employee A is a disqualified person, and Employee B is close but not a disqualified person since she is deemed to own less than 10%. Notice that the denominator for each employee only considers that employee's synthetic equity.

In this case, Company X has one disqualified person but does not have a nonallocation year because disqualified persons do not own 50% or more of the company. If we change the facts just slightly, we get a much different result.

> ***Example 13.*** Referring to table 7-4, now assume the same facts as Example 12 except that Company X is 60% owned directly by Employee A and 40% owned by the ESOP. Also, the ESOP owns 10,000 shares and Employee A owns 15,000 shares directly, for a total of 25,000 total shares outstanding.

We again have one disqualified person (Employee A is a disqualified person at 10.78%, but Employee B is not a disqualified person at only 9.36%), but now there are two big changes. The first is that the number of synthetic equity units considered outstanding for Section 409(p) purposes is reduced to reflect the ESOP's smaller ownership percentage (i.e., 40%). Section 409(p) recognizes that 60% of Company X's flow-through income is being reported to a shareholder other than a tax-exempt ESOP trust; thus, only 40% of the actual synthetic equity counts in determining disqualified persons. This generally helps an ESOP pass the test. The second big change is that you must include a disqualified person's directly owned shares in determining whether you have a nonallocation year. In this case, Employee A, a disqualified person, now owns 16,100 shares (15,000 + 900 + 200= 16,100) and in total there are 25,200 (15,000 + 10,000 + 200) shares outstanding, so Employee A is a disqualified person who owns 63.8%, and Company X has a nonallocation year and all of the problems associated with it.

Table 7-3. Example 12

	ESOP shares	Synthetic equity	Calculation	DQP percentage
Employee A	900	500	1,400 /10,500	13.33%
Employee B	900	100	1,000/10,100	9.99%
Others	8,200			
Total	10,000	600		

Table 7-4. Example 13

	Direct shares	ESOP shares	Synthetic equity	Calculation	DQP percentage
Employee A	15,000	900	500 x 40% = 200	1,100/10,200	10.78%
Employee B		900	100 x 40% = 40	940/10,040	9.36%
Others		8,200			
Total	15,000	10,000	600		

Example 13 is a real-world example typical of the planning considerations present when an owner sells only a portion of his or her shares to an ESOP. For example, the owner may receive a subordinated note in exchange for selling the shares to the ESOP and may desire some equity upside in return for the additional risks of the transaction. This often takes the form of warrants or perhaps just participation in the company's phantom stock or SAR plan. This example illustrates the careful planning required when any type of deferred compensation, be it deferred cash, actual equity awards, or equity-based awards, is added to the mix. Note that Employee A would not be a disqualified person absent the synthetic equity because Employee A then would only own 900 ESOP shares out of 10,000 ESOP shares (i.e., 9%).

Taxation of Benefits

The rules governing the taxation of qualified retirement plan benefits—such as ESOP benefits—do not apply to LTIPs. Before Section 409A was adopted, the rules governing the taxation of nonqualified deferred compensation had been a patchwork of IRS guidance and court decisions interpreting the tax doctrines of constructive receipt, economic benefit, and substantial risk of forfeiture.

Some deferred compensation plans were aggressively designed to make future payments to the recipient as accessible and secure as possible while still avoiding current income inclusion under these doctrines. In response to these aggressive designs and several high-profile company bankruptcies such as those of Enron and WorldCom, Congress in 2004 enacted Code Section 409A (effective January 1, 2005).[16]

So long as a plan subject to Code Section 409A complies with its various restrictions, recipients generally are not taxed on plan benefits until the year they receive the cash payouts or a transfer of property. However, if the plan does not comply with Section 409A, then the recipient is immediately taxed on all vested benefits, plus a 20% penalty, and interest is applied as if the deferred amounts were includible in income in the proper year. Even worse, under an aggregation rule, certain similar plans in which the recipient participates are pulled into the noncompliance net.

By statute, some plans are carved out of Section 409A, such as certain nondiscounted stock option plans and restricted stock plans. These specific plans are discussed below. Also, plans that pay deferred benefits in full in the year in which benefits vest (or within 2½ months following the end of that year) automatically satisfy Section 409A because no post-vesting deferral occurs other than a permissible short-term deferral of 2½ months.

Even if your plan pays benefits immediately upon vesting, it still is a best practice (1) to reduce all nonqualified plans to writing, (2) have the document specify that the plan is intended to be exempt from Section 409A, and (3) state that any plan provisions inconsistent with Section 409A are nullified.

As for the employer's deduction of benefits paid to the LTIP recipient, the general rules under Code Section 162 apply, as well as Code Sections 83(h) (for the transfer of property) and 404(a)(5) (for the payment of cash). In general, amounts are deductible by the employer when the amounts are includible in the LTIP recipient's income. Any tax-deferred interest or earnings credited by the employer to these amounts do not qualify as interest deductible under Section 163 but instead represent additional deferred compensation deductible under Section 404(a)(5).

---

16. The extensive regulations under Code Section 409A were adopted by the Treasury Department and became effective on January 1, 2009.

Amounts paid under the plan are usually treated as ordinary income by the recipient and are subject to FICA and tax withholding (even if the award is made entirely of stock, such as the vesting of restricted stock).[17] LTIP benefits are taken into account for FICA tax purposes at the later of (1) when the services are performed or (2) when no substantial risk of forfeiture exists on the future receipt of the deferred amounts. Thus, recipients may be subject to FICA taxation before they are subject to income taxation if the amounts are fully vested but payment is deferred.

Are interest or earnings credited to amounts deferred and paid under an LTIP subject to FICA tax as wages? Under the "non-duplication" rule, such interest or earnings may be ignored to the extent the underlying benefit already has been taxed for FICA purposes and the amount of interest or earnings being credited do not exceed a reasonable rate of return.[18]

Accounting Treatment

A complete discussion of the accounting treatment associated with LTIPs (some of which would be quite complex) is beyond the scope of this publication, but several points deserve mention.

In a typical LTIP arrangement, the future benefits payable to recipients represent liabilities of the company (rather than of a separate trust), and any amounts set aside to pay these future benefits are treated as company assets.[19]

The general accounting treatment for liabilities associated with the payment of deferred compensation is governed by FASB Accounting Standards Codification (ASC) 710-10-25 (formerly known as APB Opinion 12). Depending on the type of plan, deferred compensation could also be accounted for under ASC 715 (the former SFAS 87) if the arrangement is similar to a pension benefit and considered a "plan" instead of an individual contract.

---

17. Where the taxable award is entirely in stock, withholding on other compensation to the recipient may be required.

18. See Treas. Reg. 31.3121(v)(2)-1(a)(2)(iii).

19. Where assets are placed in a so-called "rabbi trust," the trust assets still are considered company assets and remain subject to the claims of company creditors in the event of insolvency.

The following simple example shows the accounting treatment for an individual LTIP that will pay the recipient a fixed dollar amount over the next five years.

> *Example 14.* A deferred compensation liability and a deferred compensation expense are recorded in year 1 equal to the present value of the future payments using an appropriate discount rate. The deferred compensation liability amount reduces the company's net worth on the balance sheet, while the deferred compensation expense amount reduces the company's net income on the income statement. If the benefit is contingent on future service, the liability and expense should be accrued over the vesting period.

Additional rules apply under ASC 718 (formerly known as FAS 123(R)) for share-based LTIP awards even if the award is not ultimately paid in the form of stock. The accounting treatment will differ depending on the types of equity or synthetic equity used and whether settlement of the benefit is in cash or in shares.

If the LTIP benefit is settled in stock it is considered an "equity" award for accounting purposes, with the following two primary characteristics. First, the equity accounting entry that offsets compensation expense is made to equity ("additional paid-in capital"). Second, the grant-date fair value of the award (see below) is amortized as a compensation expense over the service period, which is typically the vesting period.

The accounting for equity awards is further complicated depending on whether the award is a full-value award (like restricted stock) or an appreciation-only award (like options). For full-value equity awards, the compensation expense recognized is the underlying *stock's* fair value on the date of grant less the amount (if any) paid by the recipient.

For appreciation-only equity awards (such as options), the compensation expense recognized is the *fair value* of the *award* on the date of grant. A non-discounted option has no economic value on the date of grant since the exercise price and stock price are the same, yet we anticipate that it will have value before it expires, and the fair value of an award is determined by using an option-pricing model like Black-Scholes or a lattice model. Unfortunately, such models are notoriously difficult for privately held companies to use because there often is insufficient data to calculate the implied volatility of the stock—a key assumption in the model.

Even though it is very difficult to calculate volatility for a privately held company—even an annual appraisal history of 20 years provides limited data from a statistical standpoint—this is the expectation. A privately held company can use one of two methods to arrive at a volatility measure to use in an option-pricing model. Under the "fair value method," the company comes up with its best measure of its own volatility. Under the "calculated value method," the company creates a proxy for its volatility by creating a peer group of publicly traded companies that are in its industry or otherwise similar to the company. Of these two methods, the fair value method is preferred.

Regarding the specific amortization of the applicable compensation expense, two approaches exist if benefits are subject to a graded vesting schedule and have service vesting conditions only. Where an option vests ratably over four years (i.e., one quarter of the award vests at the end of each year), the company can amortize the compensation expense over this period on either a straight-line or graded-vesting basis. Under the straight-line method, the value of the option is divided equally over the four years. Under the graded-vesting method, each year of four-year vesting is treated as a separate award subject to its own vesting schedule so, for example, in the first year more of the award is earned than under the straight-line method, and the value expensed is front-loaded. Cliff-vested options must use the straight-line method.

Most S corporation ESOP companies use cash-settled phantom stock or stock appreciation rights (SARs), which result in so-called "liability" accounting. In liability accounting, the accounting entry that offsets the compensation expense is a liability (recall that in equity accounting the offsetting entry is to equity as additional paid-in capital).

The accounting treatment for liability awards has one major additional difference that makes it less favorable than equity awards from an accounting perspective. The value of the liability award is *remeasured at the end of each reporting period* until the award is settled in cash, meaning the award is subject to *variable* accounting during the period.

Phantom stock plans (plans that award units that track the company's actual stock price and are typically settled in cash) illustrate this liability accounting issue.

Example 15. A full-value phantom stock award vests over 5 years. If 100 units are awarded and the stock value is $5 at the end of year 1, then 20 units (one-fifth of the total) are vested, and 20 x $5 = $100 is recognized as an expense. In year 2, if the stock value is $8, then 40 units are now vested (two-fifths of the total), and $320 (40 x $8) must be recognized as the cumulative compensation expense. Since $100 has already been recognized in year 1, an additional $220 expense must be recognized in year 2. This process is repeated for each of the remaining years until the phantom stock is settled in cash. Relative to equity accounting, liability accounting produces volatility in income statements, much to the disdain of CFOs.

As noted above, the company generally cannot take a tax deduction until the employee includes the benefit in income. This means that each year the LTIP liability accrues, the company's financial accounting net income (which reflects this future liability) will be lower than its taxable income (which does not yet reflect the future compensation deduction). This creates a temporary timing difference, the so-called "book-to-tax difference."

Depending on the type of award being used, the ultimate amount of expense recognized for book financial accounting may be quite different from the amount recognized for tax purposes. The deferred income tax accounting rules of ASC 740 (formerly known as FAS 109) also may come into play for companies that are or were C corporations. Under these rules, the anticipated tax benefit of the future tax deduction will not be taken on the tax return until the employee includes the benefit in income. Any difference between the anticipated tax benefit that has been booked and the actual tax benefit is recognized in the financial statements when the actual tax benefit is realized.

Conclusion

LTIPs are used by companies to recruit, retain, reward, and even retire key employees. In terms of LTIPs linked to equity value, the applicable tax and regulatory provisions effectively winnow the LTIP options for S corporation ESOP companies down to SARs and phantom stock. Nonetheless, with proper attention to the rules, LTIPs provide considerable flexibility in determining to whom the awards are granted, how the awards are granted or vested, and how the awards are paid. Each company may have unique goals for its LTIP, yet most S corporation

ESOP companies want the LTIP to both reflect and reinforce their ownership culture and ESOP share value. Because LTIPs have so many long-term impacts on company financial statements, cash flow, and employee behavior, careful planning is advised to ensure the LTIP you get is the LTIP you want. Carpenters often quip: measure twice and cut once. A fair observation on LTIP implementation is similar: plan twice and implement once.

Chapter 8

Ownership, Motivation, and Company Performance

Corey Rosen

The tax and financial planning benefits of ESOPs are very appealing, but potentially even more powerful is their ability, through ownership sharing, to transform corporations into more motivated, innovative organizations. But does this actually happen?

In 2000, Douglas Kruse and Joseph Blasi of Rutgers University analyzed all the ESOPs set up in closely held companies between 1988 and 1994 for which data were available. They then matched these companies to comparable non-ESOP companies and looked at the sales and employment data for the paired companies for three years before the formation of the ESOP and three years after. They found that when they indexed out for the performance of the competitor companies, the ESOP companies grew 2.3% to 2.4% faster after setting up their plans than would have been expected otherwise. That seemed to give strong evidence that ESOPs do make a significant and positive contribution to corporate performance.

Impressive as these findings were, however, they did not indicate what it was about employee ownership that caused the improved performance or whether just a subset of ESOP companies with particular characteristics account for the improved performance. Other research, however, suggests that it is the combination of employee ownership and employee involvement that really makes the difference.

Knowing the answer to the question of whether ownership motivates employees seems to also answer whether employee ownership alone improves corporate performance. Not so. In most companies, labor costs are under 30% to 40% of total costs. Motivation on its own, presumably, makes employees work harder. We often ask managers to estimate just how much more work they could hope to get from more motivated employees, based on an eight-hour day. Fifteen minutes is a typical response. That comes to just 3% more time. Three percent times even a high estimate of 40% for labor costs results in just a 1.2% savings, assuming everyone will be more motivated, which is, of course, far from true.

While a 1% improvement can be a lot of money, it is not what distinguishes really successful companies from mediocre ones. The star performers are those that react to their environment in creative, innovative ways, providing better value to their customers than competitors do. How is that achieved? Through processing information and acting on it intelligently. In most companies, information gathering is limited to a group of managers. The generation of ideas is similarly limited. So is decision-making. The assumption is that only these people have the talent, and perhaps motivation, to carry out these tasks.

In fact, no one has more daily contact with customers than employees, at least in most companies. No one is closer to the day-to-day process of making the product or providing the service than the employees. And employees often do have useful ideas they could share with management.

For a company to use employee ownership effectively, it needs to do more than motivate people to work harder at what, after all, may not be the most efficient or effective thing to do. Instead, it must enlist employee ideas and information to find the best ways to do the most important things. To do that, companies need to get employees involved. Managers should seek their opinions. Employee task forces, both ad hoc and permanent, should be established to solve problems. Quality circles and employee involvement teams can be set up. Individual jobs can be enhanced, and supervision can be limited. Suggestion systems can be implemented. This all may seem like common sense, and it is. It is not very common practice in most companies, however.

Data indicate that it *is* becoming common in employee ownership companies. In a 1987 General Accounting Office (GAO) report, about one-third of all ESOP firms had some degree of employee participation. By 1993, a study of Ohio firms by the Northeast Ohio Employee Ownership Center and Kent State University found that about 60% of the companies now had active employee involvement programs, such as autonomous work teams, total quality management, or similar programs. The incidence of participation roughly doubled after the initiation of an ownership plan. These participative firms, the GAO reported, showed strong improvements in productivity when they combined their ESOPs with participative management practices.

In a study by the National Center for Employee Ownership published in the September/October 1987 *Harvard Business Review*, we found that participative ESOP firms grew 8% to 11% faster with their plans than they would have without them. In both the NCEO and GAO studies, no other factors had any influence on the relationship between ownership and performance. In 2012, Blasi, Kruse, and Richard Freeman of Harvard analyzed over 700 companies and 300,000 employee survey responses among applicants for the Best Places to Work in America list. They found again that pairing employee ownership with employee involvement programs led to significant improvements in outcome measures—in fact, more significant than any other combination of rewards and practices they looked at. Other academic studies confirmed both the direction and magnitude of these findings. Only participation can translate the motivation of ownership into the reality of a fatter bottom line. Participation is not enough on its own, however, as hundreds of studies have shown. One reason is that few participation programs last more than five years in conventional companies. In contrast, it is extremely rare in our experience for an ESOP company to drop its employee involvement program.

The structure of participation varies from company to company, but it basically boils down to employees forming groups to share information, generate ideas, and make recommendations. Taking these steps, and sticking with them, is essential.

At United Airlines, for instance, employee task teams were formed soon after the employees purchased the company. Over the ensuing two years, the teams took apart every aspect of the business, making recommendations for often-substantial changes. The teams were appointed to include a broad cross-section of employees, but anyone could volunteer to join one. The ideas helped generate hundreds of millions of dollars in cost savings and new revenues. Ironically, when the teams completed their work, management backed away from the idea of participation, causing the airline some well-reported difficulties in the years that followed. The ESOP was terminated five years later.

United shows clearly that just setting up an ESOP, and even starting off in the right direction, is not enough. Companies must commit to a long-term ownership culture.

Web Industries is great example of this process. The 500-employee company, based in Massachusetts with plants in several states, slits large pieces of plastic into small pieces of plastic for products such as diaper tapes and pull tabs for gum packs. As this business became increasingly vulnerable to low-priced overseas competition, the company enlisted its employee owners to help come up with new ideas for using their process for more value-added processes. Idea teams were formed to bring together groups of employees at every level to analyze processes, assess costs, meet with customers to explore possibilities, and develop new products. The result was contracts with several large manufacturers for very high-technology aerospace, medical technology, and other sophisticated applications. The company has been making record profits ever since, and many longer-term manufacturing employees have account balances in the hundreds of thousands of dollars.

At SRC Holdings in Springfield, Missouri, employee owners are taught to read detailed financial and production data. Meeting in work groups, they go over the numbers then figure out ways to improve them. Employees are sometimes given 90-page financial statements to digest. SRC's stock went from 10 cents a share when it started its ESOP in 1983, to over $360 in 2014. Employment increased to 1,200 employees.

Other approaches include forming committees that allow employees to advise management, eliminating levels of supervision while giving nonmanagement employees more authority, holding meetings between management and randomly selected groups of employees, placing suggestion boxes, and doing anything else companies can imagine to get people involved.

The benefits of "high-involvement" management have, of course, become conventional wisdom, if still unconventional practice, at many companies. Is ownership really essential to make it work? There are no conclusive data on this, but there is good reason to believe that ownership, if not essential, is at least highly desirable. First, ownership is a cumulative benefit. Each additional year, an employee has more and more at stake in how well the company performs. It is not unusual in mature plans for the appreciation in share value and employer contributions to add up to 30% to 50% or more of pay in a year. With profit sharing or gainsharing, both of which are paid periodically and almost always amount to a small portion of total compensation, the benefit always remains relatively minor. Second, ownership has a stronger emotive appeal. People may be very proud to say they are an owner; few would brag to friends they are a profit-sharer. Finally, only ownership encourages people to think about all aspects of a business, not just short-term profits or some efficiency measure. This is especially important in companies moving toward open-book management systems.

Chapter 9

An Integrated Framework for Sustainability in S Corporation Esops

Corey Rosen

The laws that allowed ESOPs to own S corporations and that made the profits attributable to the ESOP not subject to federal (and usually state) income taxes created a sea change in the ESOP community. Before the law, only 4% of all ESOP companies were 100% owned by the ESOP trust; today, that percentage is probably about 33%, with the percentage growing.

Because of the unique tax benefits S corporation ESOPs have, there is much more incentive than there has been in the past to remain an ESOP long-term. Moreover, as companies have moved to 100% ESOP ownership, they have become more concerned about creating and sustaining an effective ownership culture than they had been when ESOP ownership percentages were smaller. As a consequence, ESOP sustainability is a perennially popular topic at ESOP conferences. Much of the discussion focuses on internal dynamics in the ESOP, particularly:

* How to manage the repurchase obligation to make sure companies can buy back shares over time without causing excessive financial stress.

* Creating distribution policies that can balance cash flow preservation with opportunities to repurchase shares at opportune times.

* Creating rebalancing and account segregation policies to make sure that mature ESOPs can have shares to allocate to newer employees.

All of these considerations are critically important, but they are only part of the story. A truly sustainable ESOP company also has a strategy to maintain an effective employee ownership culture and a profitable business model. In particular, this means:

- Developing an effective risk management program.
- Creating a governance system consistent with being a long-term ESOP company.
- Having a leadership succession strategy to develop and promote new leaders not just at the executive level, but for all critical jobs.
- Growing an employee ownership culture of high employee involvement and open-book management.
- Implementing a corporate strategy that allows for sustainable growth, whether internally and/or through acquisitions.

This chapter discusses each of these issues. Of course, each of them merits much longer discussion on their own, so I provide references to other material that explores each topic in depth.

Managing the ESOP

Distribution Policies

ESOP distribution policies are often boilerplate insertions into plan documents that allow a company the maximum flexibility in making distributions. That means that when employees retire, die, or are disabled, the company must distribute their vested shares to them or their heirs not later than the last day of the plan year following the year of their departure. For employees leaving before reaching retirement age, distribution begins not later than the last day of the sixth plan year following the year of separation from service. C corporations can delay this distribution to terminated employees (other than when general qualified plan distribution rules mandate an earlier date, as in the case of retirement) until after the ESOP loan is repaid. Payments can be in substantially equal installments out of the trust over a period of no more than five years, or in a lump sum. In the installment method, a company normally pays out a portion of the stock from the trust each year. The value of that stock (and consequently the amount paid to the employee when the company buys back the stock) may go up or down over that time, of course. In a lump-sum distribution, the company buys the shares at their current value at the time of distribution, but it can pay for that purchase in installments over five years, as long as it provides adequate security and reasonable interest.

The logic behind this approach is that delaying the repurchase obligation as long as legally possible maximizes cash flow, allowing the company to grow rather than devote resources to repurchasing. For companies that think they will eventually be sold, delay can be a particularly good strategy because as the obligation grows in later years, someone else will take care of it when a sale occurs.

But for companies that want to stay an ESOP over the very long term, delaying repurchases may not be a good idea. If the stock value is rising faster than the company's cost of money, delay only makes the eventual costs higher. Many ESOP companies pay out sooner than required, based on that theory and/or a desire to make the ESOP seem more relevant to people by showing them that they will not have to wait as long to get their money.

In an attempt to balance the desire to hold on to cash and the appeal of limiting future obligations if share prices rise quickly, some ESOP companies adopt a written distribution policy that exists outside the plan document. If distribution policies exist only in the document, the plan must be amended any time it is changed. If the document provides that the shares will be repurchased not later than in the maximum allowed periods but that a separate written distribution policy will provide the specific rules, that policy can be more liberal than the plan document requires and can be changed without a plan amendment.

The ESOP committee or other body deciding on the distribution policy could be given some discretion to make payouts sooner than required. There are many possible variations on this. The plan might say that people with under a certain dollar amount (but one above the legal minimums) would be cashed out sooner, or that people at some age earlier than retirement age would be cashed out, or that everyone would be cashed out in some period less than the required periods. To protect cash flow, however, the plan would give the committee discretion to delay payouts on a nondiscriminatory basis if the cash requirements of early payouts would put the company at financial risk.

Legal opinion is divided on this approach. Some advisors say that discretion is per se a problem. Others say that if a company follows the same rules every year, it has created a de facto policy that employees should be able to rely on. Many others, however, say that this approach is reasonable and in the best long-term interests of plan participants as long as it is done in a way that scrupulously avoids favoring more highly compensated participants.

Another issue is who should repurchase the shares. Contributions made to the ESOP to buy back shares are tax-deductible, whereas corporate redemptions are not. (However, this tax advantage is irrelevant for a 100% ESOP-owned S corporation due to the absence of taxes in that case.) The contributions are allocated to employee accounts, however, creating an additional long-term repurchase liability compared to retiring the shares. The company can repurchase the shares and then recontribute them to the ESOP trust. The advantage here is that the company can smooth out annual contributions based on a target percentage of pay rather than basing annual contributions at least in part on the ups and downs of how many shares need to be bought back by the ESOP each year. The company would contribute the needed shares each year and hold the rest in reserve; in a year with a lower repurchase level, it might add some of those shares to the repurchased shares for the annual contribution.

As noted above, in a 100% ESOP-owned S corporation there is no tax advantage to contributing money to the ESOP to buy back shares. Buying them back at the corporate level and recontributing them as needed, therefore, generally is a better idea. Some S corporation ESOPs have substantial accumulated cash distributions on the trust, especially if they were once partially owned by the ESOP and had to make pro-rata distributions to the plan because they made them to other S corporation owners. These companies may be able to handle a large part of their repurchase obligation with these funds, at least for some years.

No one policy will be most sustainable for every company. Companies need to perform regular repurchase analyses and consult with their advisors to come up with a plan that works best. That plan needs periodic review if circumstances change.

Rebalancing and Account Segregation

As ESOPs mature, they can develop a "have/have-not" problem that makes sustaining an ownership culture very difficult. Employees in the early years may have benefitted from large annual contributions used to acquire company stock. Once all the shares are acquired, new employees get shares only from forfeitures or recycled repurchased shares. That may not be enough to give them a real sense of ownership.

At the design phase, companies can help void this problem if the internal ESOP loan does not have an excessively short term. If all the shares are paid for over 5 years, for instance, the problem will become much larger faster than if the internal loan is for 10 years. Extending the term of internal loan beyond 10 years may raise fiduciary issues, however, unless there is a compelling reason to do so (such as needing to keep within the annual contribution limits).

Many ESOP companies now address the have/have-not problem with account segregation and/or rebalancing accounts.

Account segregation is the simplest. It provides that when employees terminate, their account balances are transferred to cash until their distribution begins. While that means companies have the money to cash people out right away, many prefer not to because it can give employees an incentive to leave. As an example of segregation, say the company has a five-year waiting period before distribution begins. An employee leaves the company, and the ESOP administrator calculates that the employee's vested account balance is worth $50,000. The plan can invest the cash equivalent of the value in other investments until the distribution begins.

When using account segregation, the employee's consent to distribution must not impose a "significant detriment on a participant who does not consent to distribution." That means that plan must provide a reasonable and prudent menu of investment options for the cash, such as at least three different investment choices including a life-cycle fund or target-date fund. Some companies now simply put the cash in some very conservative investment, such as a CD. That would not appear acceptable under this guidance.

With rebalancing, at the end of each plan year, the company uses cash in the accounts of employees with cash to buy shares from those with shares in such a way that at the end of the procedure, everyone has the same percentage of stock and cash (subject to some limitations described below). In 2010, the IRS made it clear that this is allowable, provided certain rules are met. The plan document must allow for this.

To illustrate rebalancing, say John has $10,000, all in cash, and Mary has $100,000, all in stock. Overall, 80% of plan assets are in company stock. The trustee would buy and sell shares within the trust so that John would now have $2,000 in cash and $8,000 in stock and Mary $80,000 in stock and $20,000 in cash. Another common approach is "profit sharing" accounting. In this model, the trust holds all the assets and employees have a percentage interest in the total assets, with each employee having the same percentage of shares and other investments as each other employee.

The IRS made several key points to keep in mind for rebalancing:

1. There must be a written program in the plan to set out a "definite predetermined allocation formula." That should include the number of shares (presumably a formula that will be applied in each year to arrive at the number) and the manner in which the transfer will be effectuated, including the applicable valuation date.

2. The right of each participant to have a particular form of investment does not raise the problematic issue of "effective availability of benefits" so long as all participants are treated in the same way. (For segregation, because these participants are a separate class of employee, nondiscriminatory reshuffling also does not affect current availability.)

3. The right to retain employer stock is not a protected benefit. However, the rebalancing cannot be done in such a way that someone who has diversified his or her account into cash now will have some of that cash moved back into stock.

Another approach that is less common but increasingly discussed is refinancing the ESOP. A new ESOP loan would be taken out to buy back some or all the shares in the plan. These shares then get allocated to all current employees based on the allocation formula. This can work well for companies with strong cash flow. The new debt can affect existing share value, however, and companies need to decide whether they want to ameliorate a drop in share value through price protection, a subject beyond the scope of this chapter.

Valuation

One of the most important issues affecting sustainability is making sure the repurchase obligation is reflected in the appraisal. In the past, it rarely was. Appraisers argued that ESOP companies could always be purchased to make the obligation go away. Of course, if an ESOP company wants to be an ESOP in the long term, this is not a helpful argument. Meanwhile, some lawyers and fiduciaries argued that since a willing buyer would always make the obligation go away, and the sale is based on what a willing buyer would pay, the repurchase obligation should generally be ignored.

In recent years, however, the consensus has strongly shifted so that almost all institutional fiduciaries and most lawyers and appraisers believe that the repurchase obligation should be a factor. There are many different models for this, but basically they all ask whether the obligation creates an additional cash flow obligation beyond what the company would otherwise need to contribute to its benefit plans. Ignoring this impact, which can be substantial or minimal depending on a variety of factors, means that people who leave sooner get paid based on cash flow assumptions that are more optimistic than what will be the case for those who leave later. In some cases, the effect may be to push the appraisal high enough so that if the company hits a down cycle and is paying off employees on an installment plan or in a lump sum based on last year's price, the company could be forced into a cash flow crisis. Because of these issues, it seems prudent for an ESOP fiduciary to insist that repurchase be considered if the ESOP is meant to be a long-term plan.

Ownership Culture

In the mid-1980s, the NCEO did an extensive research project on what makes some ESOP companies perform better than others. The answer was clear: the best-performing companies had extensive employee involvement systems—open-book management, employee teams, ad-hoc employee problem-solving groups, and other structured ways to get employees to contribute ideas. Open-door policies were not enough. Effective communications about the ESOP mattered but were not sufficient. The most participative ESOP companies improved their post-ESOP performance by 6% to 11% per year over what would have been expected; the least participative ones, which had raised employee expectations about their role in the company but not met them, actually showed a decline in performance.

When this research came out, many people in the ESOP community were skeptical, but repeated studies on the same issue have come to the same conclusion and, more persuasively, the stories of successful ESOP companies described in newsletters and meetings convinced just about everyone that a high-engagement culture was essential to making ESOPs succeed over the long run.

Ownership culture does need to start, however, with communications. People need to know what an ESOP is (and isn't). Many companies start out well enough. They hold a company-wide meeting, pass out materials, solicit questions, and maybe set up an FAQ site on their Web site. Not as many companies, however, sustain that commitment over time.

The best communications programs have a few key characteristics:

1. They provide frequent small bites of information. A company might have a piece on ESOPs in each newsletter, or a monthly email, or a one-page explanation of some aspect of ESOPs every month it sends to people. These small chunks of information are easier to digest. The regular repetition, however, is itself a powerful communication tool reminding people about being an ESOP company.

2. They have an ESOP communications committee or team that includes nonmanagement employees who develop approaches that are well-suited to the particular population.

3. They have an orientation to the ESOP program for new employees and invite existing ones who want a refresher to sit in.

4. They use multiple modes of communication. Some people learn visually, others by reading, others by having discussions.

5. They make communications as interactive as possible. For instance, a company might have a program on its site that lets people plug in some realistic numbers to see how their accounts might grow over time. Others have some kind of ESOP game at annual meetings, such as ESOP Jeopardy, to get people thinking about the ESOP.

6. They celebrate and have fun.

Communications is just the start, however. Companies need to create and sustain an ownership culture. We at the NCEO have found there are six key elements to this culture:

1. Provide a financially meaningful ownership stake, enough to be an important part of employee financial security.

2. Provide ownership education that teaches people how the company makes money and their role in making that happen.

3. Share performance data about how the company is doing overall and how each work group contributes to that.

4. Train people in business literacy so they understand the numbers the company shares.

5. Share profits through bonuses, profit sharing, or other tools.

6. Build employee involvement not just by allowing employees to contribute ideas and information but making that part of their everyday work organization through teams, feedback opportunities, devolution of authority, and other structures.

ESOP companies that succeed do so because they develop cultures that engage employees to generate lots of new ideas all the time, small and large. It is these new ideas that really move a company forward. Getting people more motivated to do what they already do but faster or more carefully is useful, but its impact on the bottom line, research consistently shows, pales compared to the impact of ideas. Some companies generate and implement hundreds or even thousands of new ideas each year.

Different companies take different approaches to generating employee ideas. At Phelps County Bank in Rolla, Missouri, employee engagement started with training all employees about banking, including material that might normally only be used with potential managers. A "problem-busting" committee was formed consisting of representative employees. Anyone with an idea or a problem could make a suggestion to the committee, which would then either act on it right away, pass it on to management, or set up an ad hoc committee to come to a decision. Anyone could be on the committee who wanted to join, but the problem-busting committee would also designate some people. Over time, the process became so much part of Phelps culture that formal structure was no longer needed—employees just took it on themselves to form the committees.

Other companies, such as Reflexite and Foldcraft, both mid-sized manufacturers, took the process one step further and created a form for people to fill out to identify a problem or idea in more detail. The process was not closed until the person submitting the form agreed the resolution from the steering committee handling it was satisfactory. A key insight of all three companies was that employee ideas do not always have to be suggestions for improvement. They can also just identify a problem. After all, if the gas is leaking, but someone does not know how to turn it off, should your policy be "if you don't have an idea to fix it, don't bother me?"

Other companies have more formal systems, such as the Great Game of Business, pioneered by SRC Holdings, that is keyed around regular meetings of all staff at all levels to review a whole set of metrics, financial and non-financial, then come up with ideas on how to improve performance. At Recology, a waste management company based in the San Francisco Bay Area, a series of 12 conferences for all 2,100 employees was used to go through a detailed process that got every employee to come up with an idea for improving the company. Small groups met to discuss the ideas, which went back to the whole group. These were collected and, generally, implemented. Walman Optical set up "innovation committees" to look at all the company processes to identify ways to improve performance. Many ESOP committees have work teams throughout the company that meet on a regular basis to discuss operations in their areas, as well as cross-functional teams to discuss issues such as safety, wellness, project development, and so on.

No one structure will be right for every company. It is not unusual for a company to start a participation process only to see it fail early on because it is not well suited to the needs of the employees and the company. Companies need to create a process to review their approaches and find what does work—and reevaluate it regularly to see what might work better. The key is that to generate ideas, companies need specific structures that make idea generation not just something employees can do but something that is part of their everyday job.

It is also essential to periodically revisit, revise, and reinvigorate ownership culture. Success can breed complacency, but it is essential to remember that new employees will not just automatically "get it." Extensive orientation programs, mentoring, and ongoing communications can help new employees understand the ESOP, but companies also need to know that even the most effective employee involvement and open-book systems can become stale and/or fail to take advantage of new ideas and technologies for moving culture forward. Companies need an ongoing team to evaluate and change ownership culture as needed.

Leadership Succession

No company is sustainable unless it has a leadership succession and development policy that works. Many people think of leadership succession in terms of CEOs and a few other corporate officers, but leadership succession also matters throughout the company among any employees who can assume leadership roles—supervisors, team leaders, and key technical people, for instance.

It is always important, of course, that new leaders have the specific skills needed for their jobs. But most leaders in an ESOP company need cultural skills as well. They need to genuinely buy into the company's ownership culture. If the company is the kind of open-book, high-engagement culture described above, leaders need to see the nurturing of that culture as one of the most essential elements of their jobs. Many CEOs we at the NCEO have spoken to say it is the most essential element.

This is not an easy hurdle for leaders to meet. The kinds of people who rise in organizations often are very self-confident, sure about their ideas, and good at getting other people to follow their lead. Those are important traits, but they can make people less receptive to and patient with the ideas of other people. The leaders who most succeed in getting others engaged also are humble. They do not assume they have the best ideas or that their title or achievements mean their ideas automatically deserve more weight. They are eminently approachable and available. They are secure enough in their own sense of self-worth and achievement that they do not need to compete with other people to show that their ideas are usually best.

Finding these people from outside the organization is a challenge. Anyone smart enough to be seriously considered for a top leadership job is probably smart enough to know to say the right things in an interview about how they would act within the company's cultural framework. But unless they have a record of leading this way, it is difficult to know how much credibility to put in these statements. On the flip side, however, an ESOP company might have current leaders who rose up in the pre-ESOP days. They may be good at their jobs and treat people well, but if open-door policies and employee engagement were not on the agenda before the ESOP, they may not put it there after the ESOP is implemented, although leaders often are transformed as they get involved in the ESOP community and see the power of ownership culture. But if that does not happen, these leaders need to be replaced with new ones who do buy in to the culture.

So how can companies test for cultural fit? If an employee has been working for the company, this should not be difficult because there is a track record. Of course, how management views that track record for other managers may not be the same as how employees view it. When the NCEO first studied employee ownership cultures, we found that nonmanagement employees invariably thought they had less say in the company than managers thought they had no matter how the company ranked in overall engagement. When asked to rate how much say employees had in various matters on a seven-point scale, managers almost invariably provided a number one point higher than employees did, no matter how strong the company's engagement program actually was. One way to get a broader idea on how effective potential leaders are in terms of ownership culture is to involve nonmanagement employees in vetting leadership candidates. That could be done through an interview process with an ESOP committee or 360-degree reviews, for instance.

Of course, for some jobs, such as CFO, ownership culture skills are less essential to the position and may not need to be high on the list of candidate evaluation. But it is important that at least these people not act to undermine the culture.

While succession is important, companies also need to focus on leadership development. One of the lessons of great employee ownership companies is that they are open to the idea that lots of people can assume leadership skills. They rely less on tracking systems that put certain people on certain paths. They realize that sometimes people hired for very different jobs can become great leaders in very different areas. Colleen Barrett, the former CEO of Southwest Airlines, a company with a long-standing employee ownership plan, started out as a secretary.

Great employee ownership companies also realize that some people have great skills at their jobs, but are not cut out to be leaders. There is a tendency to want to reward top performers by moving them up to managerial positions they may neither want nor be good at. For instance, in one ESOP company, a star employee developed a significant new product line that generates impressive margins and growth. She was offered a management job but was so unsettled by the idea that she said she would rather quit. Instead, the company found other ways to create a title and pay level for her that reflected her contributions but did not require moving up a corporate ladder. In fact, the best employee ownership companies try to get away from ladders at all. W.L. Gore and Associates has no hierarchy or titles at all—and over 8,000 employees. It lets anyone become a leader who can convince enough people to join a project team. They are then leaders for that idea. Half the workforce has been a leader at one time or another.

Great employee ownership companies also do not just think of leadership succession at the management level. They create ownership succession strategies for the whole company. The NCEO's publication *Leadership Development and Succession*[1] profiles two very successful ESOP companies, BL Companies and SRC Holdings.

BL Companies, a 100% ESOP-owned engineering, architecture, and land survey company with over 250 employees, looks at any position

---

1. Keith Boatright, Edmund B. Freeman, Amy Lyman, and Corey Rosen, *Leadership Development and Succession* (Oakland, CA: NCEO, 2012); see nceo.org/r/leadership for details.

where the loss of the person filling it would create significant pain. The company developed a competency map of eight key behaviors (accountability, teamwork, developing others, relationship building, client focus, communication, strategic thinking, and leading and managing change). Over a few years, the company rolled out a development program that touched everyone in the company. The competency map started at the hiring process, with periodic reviews on how they performed against the competency measures. A "BL Leadership Foundations Program" created a two-day program focused on developing key leader skills around ownership culture. Participants took an emotional IQ test and discussed the results. Eventually, over 50 people took part in the program. Senior leaders are provided ongoing coaching and a 360-degree assessment. Additional learning programs are provided on an ongoing basis for senior leaders.

The program succeeded in identifying positions at all levels that would need eventual replacement, finding at least two potential candidates for each position, and providing the education and mentoring needed to make these new leaders effective.

SRC Holdings (formerly Springfield ReManufacturing) is a 100% ESOP-owned, 1,200-employee company that became an ESOP when employees bought it in 1983 to prevent it from closing. There were 119 employees at the time. SRC developed the Great Game of Business, a comprehensive and much-lauded open-book management program. It also created what may be the most thoroughgoing leadership development and succession program we at the NCEO have seen.

Twice each year, the HR team meets to identify all key positions, defined as executives, managers, critical technical people, and promising associates at all levels. They then look at who holds all those positions now, mapping out how they might be needed over the next few years. Three potential candidates for each position are identified. Generally, the people in each key position are responsible for identifying these individuals. In each case, key skills are identified. For the candidates, each person is evaluated who is ready now, who might be ready in a year or two, and who might be ready in more than two years. Each of these people gets an individual; development plan to help them develop the skills they will need. These are tracked and evaluated regularly. The HR team uses its semiannual meetings to review the process and identify talent gaps that may need to be filled outside of those who have been identified, including possibly hiring people from outside the company. The process can also identify people who do not need to move up but move laterally to other jobs that need their talents.

BL and SRC have impressive systems, and not every company will want or feel the need to do anything quite as elaborate, but their core ideas of leadership development as an organization-wide process with substantial resources devoted to it helps create sustainable success, both by making sure key positions are filled by the right people and by giving employees a sense that there are a lot of opportunities to move ahead.

Governance

As ESOP companies have started more to think of being employee-owned as a long-term objective, they have also started to focus more on what kinds of governance structures will work best for them. In the past, ESOP companies were governed not much differently from any private company, with boards made up of insiders and/or family members and corporate officers serving as plan fiduciaries. While this is still true for many ESOP companies, a growing number are adding outside board members and independent trustees. There are good arguments to be made over whether independent plan fiduciaries are critical to sustainability, but there is a broad consensus among ESOP advisors that having outside board members is a good idea.

The most recent (2012) NCEO governance survey as of this writing found that 62% of the 502 respondents had at least one outside director, and half of these had three or more outsiders. Thirty-eight percent of the respondents had an executive compensation committee composed solely of outsiders.

There are several arguments for having outsiders on a board:

- Outsiders provide credibility for employees that the company takes being employee-owned seriously.

- Well-chosen outsiders can offer special expertise, insights, and/or business contacts.

- Outside board members can help make sure executive pay policies are appropriate.

- The presence of outside board members can transform board meetings from brief rubber stamps of management initiatives into serious discussion and review, often resulting in new ideas.

We at the NCEO have seen a number of examples of this process at work. For instance, outside board members:

- Led a company to change its sales compensation from revenue-driven to margin-driven, resulting in substantially higher profits.
- Created a formal review policy for CEO and top executive compensation that resulted in a revised structure for pay that was more incentive-based.
- Got management to start a risk assessment review and set up a process to deal with potential threats.
- Helped to start an idea-generating process deep in the company.
- Mediated between family member owners at odds over the future of the company.

In choosing outside board members, there are several possible areas of expertise to look for. As a result, ideally a company has between two and four outsiders. One or two might have industry expertise and contacts. Another may have expertise on employee ownership and/or employee engagement. Another may be an outsider to the industry but have entrepreneurial and leadership skills that can help leadership think of new approaches to the business.

Most boards meet four times per year in person, with committee meetings in between as needed. In addition to financial data, board members should read and review the annual valuation. (Note that some independent ESOP fiduciaries object to sharing the report on the basis that it is written solely for them, so it is important to have this discussion beforehand.)

They should meet with the plan trustee once a year to go over ESOP operations and issues, such as emerging repurchase needs. Finally, board members should have opportunities to meet with nonmanagement employees. This can be through lunches at annual meetings, having a few employees make presentations as each meeting, or setting up a specific meeting with a group of employees outside of the formal board meeting.

Companies also need to provide board members with appropriate training, both as to their fiduciary duties as board members but also the special issues ESOPs create. Finally, boards should develop specific written policies on how they will respond to a potential acquirer. The policy should be sent to any serious acquirer and indicate what information will be needed, describe the process the board and the trustee (if the offer gets that far) will go through, and, if appropriate, make a statement about the company desiring to maintain its status as an employee ownership company. Of course, the board cannot refuse any and all offers, but a written policy such as this will deter all but the most determined and aggressive potential buyers, meaning the company will be sold when it wants to be sold.

The issue of whether to have an independent trustee is not as clear cut. Forty-four percent of the respondents in the NCEO survey mentioned above said they had an outside trustee, but this dropped to 25% in companied with revenues of under $50 million. About half the outside trustees were directed by an internal ESOP committee.

The arguments for an independent, outside trustee focus on three key issues:

- They do not present the same potential problem of a conflict of interest that an insider has. Courts look to process, not results, in evaluating ESOP cases, and an independent outside trustee helps make the argument that the process was set up to protect employee interests.

- They can lend substantial expertise to decisions about the ESOP ranging from plan operations to valuation to executive compensation.

- They can make the ESOP seem more credible to employees.

When a company directs its outside trustees, the conflict of interest argument goes away. The courts will consider the person causing the decision to be made the actual fiduciary, although directed trustees still must assure that any decisions do not violate ERISA or plan rules. Generally, that means the outside trustees will give great deference to instructions, but not a carte blanche. The directed trustee in these cases plays more of a role of expert advisor.

The arguments against outside trustees focus on three points:

- Outside trustees are costly, ranging anywhere from $20,000 per year and up.

- Independent trustees may make decisions leadership would not, particularly about a sale of the company (in practice, this has been exceedingly rare, however).

- The risk of being sued at all, much less successfully, is very small. Only about a dozen ESOP cases in closely held companies make it to court each year. (Department of Labor audits are far more common, however, and, in a few cases, having an independent trustee might help reach a better outcome if the Department does find a violation.)

We at the NCEO do not believe there is a right or wrong answer to this question. We do believe, however, that there are some best practices for inside trustees:

- Generally, a committee of trustees is a better approach because it brings one or more sets of eyes to make sure the appraisal is done correctly, the plan is operated according to the plan rules, and shareholder responsibilities are followed on issues such as offers, acquisitions of other companies, and making sure executive pay is not egregious.

- Inside fiduciaries need to spend significant time being trained about ESOPs, including reading materials developed for this purpose, attending Webinars, and going to conferences.

- Inside fiduciaries need to be especially vigilant about reading, understanding, and, where appropriate, questioning, the appraisal. It is not enough simply to accept what the appraiser recommends.

Strategy and Risk Management

ESOP companies are no different from any other companies in needing to develop appropriate short- and long-term strategies and approaches to risk management. They need to add to the mix, however, how the repurchase obligation will affect strategy, how potential acquisitions will fit into the corporate culture, how layoffs will be handled, and other factors that make ESOP companies different.

Strategy and risk management are large issues far beyond this brief overview. The following can just illustrate a few key issues to suggest how ESOP companies might react to them differently. In each case, the key is that ESOP company boards and managers need to explicitly look at the effects of the ESOP in making their decisions.

Risk Management

ESOP companies may be more cautious in managing risk than other companies. Many ESOP company boards are reluctant to make risky decisions concerning growth, for instance, for fear that the costs may impinge on their ability to handle the repurchase obligation. While this is a legitimate concern, risk aversion can mean missing substantial opportunities for the kind of profitable growth that not only benefits all employee owners but makes handling repurchases easier. While there is no obvious rule of thumb, ESOP companies can make more informed risk decisions if they are clear that reasonable alternative projections for repurchase obligations are based on varying growth assumptions over a three- to five-year period. The company should have a high level of certainty that it can fund the repurchase obligation in various likely scenarios.

Layoffs

Data from the General Social Survey[2] suggest that ESOP companies lay people off at about one-third to one-fourth the rate of non-ESOP companies. Other research shows that ESOP companies tend to be "stickier" in both hiring and laying people off, hiring fewer in upturns and laying off fewer in downturns.

---

2. The General Social Survey, conducted by the National Opinion Research Center at the University of Chicago, is a widely used sociological survey that collects data on demographic characteristics and attitudes of United States residents.

The preference for employment stability makes a great deal of sense in an ESOP company. If employees feel their jobs are more secure, they will be much more willing to become fully engaged participants in ownership cultures, making them more likely to think of new ideas, work efficiently, and encourage their peers to act like owners as well.

But ESOP companies are not immune to economic cycles and can and do face a need to cut back. Some ESOP companies have set up a process for what happens when the company is economically challenged. That may start with non-employment cost reductions, followed if needed by additional steps that implement reductions in hours worked, voluntary pay cuts, job sharing, and, if all else fails, layoffs. Companies with more of a cushion may pay people whose jobs are no longer needed to learn other jobs in the company. Hypertherm, a 100% ESOP-owned, 1,300 employee manufacturer in New Hampshire, has a decades-old no-layoff policy and used downturns to cross-train employees, perform additional maintenance, and/or look for new business opportunities.

Acquisitions

Most mature ESOP-owned S corporations either have done one or more acquisitions or are considering them. The tax benefit these companies receive provides a potentially substantial cash reserve that can be used to buy other companies.

All the usual issues apply when considering an acquisitions, but ESOP companies also need to consider whether the acquired employees will be part of the ESOP (ERISA rules may often require that), whether other benefits will be integrated in the plans of the parent, and how the acquisitions can be structured to maximize tax benefits to the seller (and, as a result, provide an opportunity to buy the company at a lower price). In addition, there are critical cultural issues:

- Will management roles be integrated and, if so, how?

- How should companies deal with managers at the acquired firm who do not buy into the idea of an ownership culture (for instance, prefer more directive management)?

- How will the ESOP be communicated to acquired employees and, as critically, to employees of the parent?

- Should the company attempt to change the ownership culture practices of the acquired company, and, if so, how? Extending financial information sharing may seem a relatively simple thing to do, but what about such things as how (or whether) employee teams are used?

Research shows that poor cultural integration is the major cause of failures in acquisitions. ESOP companies have both a challenge and opportunity on this front. Employees of the acquired firm may welcome the chance to be more involved in how their work as done, creating new opportunities for growth the prior employer could not realize. But there can also be a lot of resistance, especially at the mid-management level, to any kind of change that diminishes authority or is simply different. A good first step early on is to create a joint ownership culture transition team with people from various areas and levels on the parent and target firm to plan for transition.

Involving Employees Below the Top Management Level

Some ESOP companies have structures to involve nonmanagement employees in organizational strategy. This can have a number of benefits:

- It can make ownership seem more real to employees at all levels if they see peers involved in these matters.
- Nonmanagement employees may have a more realistic view of how strategic changes will work on the everyday employee level, raising potential challenges and opportunities management cannot see.
- Employees may have their own ideas about opportunities for growth that are well worth considering.

Companies that do this need a process, typically involving employee teams designated for these purposes. At Web Industries Hartford, for instance, employee teams meet periodically to review all new business opportunities. They meet directly with customers to see what the customers might need as part of this process. The teams will generate a variety of new ideas over the course of a year and, at the end of the year, employees meet in random groups to go over the best ideas from each team, narrowing them down to a smaller list of "should do" projects.

Management could veto the projects, but the expectation is that the teams have the authority to make their own decisions. Their approach has been enormously successful, making Web one of the most innovative ESOP manufacturing firms.

Conclusion

As more and more ESOP companies plan to stay employee-owned (or have been) for decades, sustaining ownership in a way that is financially manageable and culturally effective requires a great deal of time and work. The popularity of this topic at employee ownership meetings is indicative of just how much there is to know. But given the extraordinary tax benefits of an ESOP-owned S corporation, plus the demonstrated impact of a strong ownership culture, it is clear to companies that sustaining an ESOP long-term is well worth the effort.

About the Authors

Kathryn F. Aschwald, CFA, ASA, and **Donna J. Walker,** CFA, FASA, are principals and founding shareholders of Columbia Financial Advisors, Inc., a business appraisal and financial advisory firm headquartered in Portland, Oregon. Columbia Financial Advisors, Inc., is nationally recognized for its expertise in ESOP appraisal and financial advisory services. Ms. Aschwald is a member of the ESOP Association's Valuation Advisory Committee and is a past chair of that committee and was a founding member (2006–2010) of the ESOP Association's Interdisciplinary Committee on Fiduciary Issues. Ms. Walker is the course developer for the American Society of Appraisers' ESOP valuation course. Both Ms. Aschwald and Ms. Walker have significant experience in ESOP-related appraisal and fairness issues and are frequent speakers, lecturers, and teachers on the subject of ESOP appraisal and financial advice.

Barbara M. Clough, QPA, QKA, is a managing director at Blue Ridge ESOP Associates, a nationally recognized third-party administration firm, which provides employee benefit plan administration and related services exclusively to ESOP companies. During Ms. Clough's tenure in the qualified plan administration field, she has been the ESOP manager for a mid-sized consulting firm and responsible for the training and oversight of a staff of 12 administrators. Her administration experience includes plans at private and publicly held companies ranging in size from 20 to 20,000 employees as well as extensive experience with ERISA law, Department of Labor regulations, Internal Revenue Code compliance, and IRS/DOL audits. Ms. Clough has worked closely with plan sponsors, accountants, and legal counsel to provide guidance on plan design, resolution of legal and compliance matters, and audit discrepancies. Ms. Clough holds a bachelor of science degree from the University of Massachusetts. She is the current chair of the ESOP Association's Administrative Advisory Committee, a past administration representative on the ESOP Association's Interdisciplinary Committee, the vice president of programming for the New England Chapter of the ESOP Association, and a frequent author and speaker at NCEO and ESOP Association conferences. Ms. Clough is a member of ASPPA, the ESOP Association, and NCEO.

Brian D. Hector is a partner in the employee benefits and executive compensation practice of Morgan, Lewis & Bockius LLP, and is chair of the firm's ESOP task force. He focuses his practice on ERISA and employee benefits law, including the areas of ESOPs, qualified plans, all types of executive compensation, fiduciary liability, and related securities law issues. He is a nationally recognized ESOP attorney who has advised several public and private ESOP companies with regard to corporate governance, succession planning strategies, ownership transition, and liquidity transactions. Mr. Hector has served as counsel to companies and shareholders regarding the use of ESOPs in many transactions, including equity repurchases, ownership succession transactions, leveraged buyouts, mergers, acquisitions, and corporate reorganizations. He has also represented lenders and trustees in ESOP transactions. He has also represented several clients before the IRS and the Department of Labor in connection with ESOP and employee benefits matters. Mr. Hector has lectured extensively regarding employee benefits and ESOPs. He speaks regularly at the annual national conferences of the ESOP Association and the National Center for Employee Ownership, at their local and regional conferences, and at many other seminars. Mr. Hector is also an adjunct professor at John Marshall Law School, teaching in the area of employee benefits law.

Matthew G. Keene is a managing director at Chartwell Capital Solutions, where he leads the firm's executive compensation consulting practice. He works with private companies to obtain relevant pay data and achieve key goals for their compensation systems, with a special focus on ESOP companies and equity-based incentives. Over the past decades he has worked with companies on all aspects of qualified and nonqualified plan origination, operation, and termination. Before joining Chartwell, Matt spent 10 years with a leading ESOP administration and consulting firm, and before that he spent 12 years with a Big Four accounting firm, where he worked in the national tax department. He frequently writes and speaks on executive compensation and participates in various capacities with the ESOP Association, the NCEO, and the National Association of Stock Plan Professionals. Matt received a BS in business administration and a master of accounting from the University of North Carolina at Chapel Hill.

Thomas Roback, Jr., CEP, QKA, is a managing director at Blue Ridge ESOP Associates. Tom has worked in the accounting, investment, and ESOP industry for over 17 years. He is an expert in the design, implementation, and execution of ESOP, stock option, stock purchase, and restricted stock plans. Mr. Roback received his MBA from the University of Baltimore and a BS in accounting from the College of William and Mary. He is a Qualified 401(k) Administrator, Certified Equity Professional, and Capital Area regional vice president of the ESOP Association's Mid-Atlantic Chapter. He is a member of the ESOP Association and the NCEO.

Corey Rosen is the founder and former executive director of the National Center for Employee Ownership (NCEO) and now is its senior staff member. He cofounded the NCEO in 1981 after working for five years as a professional staff member in the U.S. Senate, where he helped draft legislation on employee ownership plans. Before that, he taught political science at Ripon College. He is the author or coauthor of over 100 articles and many books on employee ownership, and a coauthor (with John Case and Martin Staubus) of *Equity: Why Employee Ownership Is Good for Business* (Harvard Business School Press, 2005). He has lectured on employee ownership on six continents, has appeared frequently on CNN, PBS, NPR, MSNBC, and other network programs, and is regularly quoted in the *Wall Street Journal,* the *New York Times, Business Week,* and other leading publications. He holds a PhD in political science from Cornell University.

Carolyn Zimmerman is a past member of the board of directors of the ESOP Association and past chair of the ESOP Association's Advisory Committee Chairs Council. Before entering the ESOP world, she spent 10 years in the financial services industry, where she began dealing with ERISA plans in 1985. She holds a BA from Duke University and an MLS from Columbia University (New York City).

About the NCEO

The National Center for Employee Ownership (NCEO) is widely considered to be the leading authority on employee ownership in the U.S. and the world. Established in 1981 as a nonprofit information and membership organization, it now has over 2,500 members, including companies, professionals, unions, government officials, academics, and interested individuals. It is funded entirely through the work it does.

The NCEO's mission is to provide the most objective, reliable information possible about employee ownership at the most affordable price possible. As part of the NCEO's commitment to providing objective information, it does not lobby or provide ongoing consulting services. The NCEO publishes a variety of materials on employee ownership and participation; holds dozens of seminars, Webinars, and conferences on employee ownership annually; and offers online courses. The NCEO's work also includes extensive contacts with the media, both through articles written for trade and professional publications and through interviews with reporters.

Membership Benefits

NCEO members receive the following benefits:

- The members-only newsletter *Employee Ownership Report.*
- Access to the members-only area of the NCEO's Web site.
- Free access to live Webinars.
- Discounts on books and other NCEO products and services.
- The right to contact the NCEO for answers to questions.

An introductory one-year membership costs $90 for U.S. residents. To join or order publications, telephone us at 510-208-1300 or visit our Web site at www.nceo.org, which provides news updates and hundreds of articles as well as information on the many ways in which we can assist companies exploring employee ownership.